A Leper's Tale

the story of Naaman

William G. Collins

Cover art: Naaman the Leper

Eikon Bible Art: Used with permission:

Cover design: Whiterabbitgraphix – Christine Holmes

ISBN: 0692438084

ISBN 13: 9780692438084

"…and there were many in Israel with leprosy
in the time of Elisha the prophet—
yet not one of them was cleansed—
only **Naaman the Syrian***."*

The words of Jesus
Luke 4:27

DEDICATION

For all who love the stories of the Bible.

ACKNOWLEDGMENTS

To my wife, Evangeline Rose, whose sharp eye and knowledge
of grammar keep me from many a disaster.
To the Port Orange Scribes of the
Florida Writer's Association: Peggy Lambert, Leader.
J. W. Thompson, Terri Curtis, Michael Murray, Joan J. Harris,
Joyce Senatro, Mary Kay Pyles,
Ben Seeley, Diane Boilard, and Walter Doherty.
Without their support and encouragement, and
infinite patience with ancient names and customs,
this book could not have been written.

PREFACE

When I was a boy the story of Naaman the Syrian was one of the most exciting and rewarding adventures of the Bible. There were many surprises as I researched the kind of life he must have led as General and Commander of Hadadezer's armed forces. The Israelites called this king Ben Hadad because Jewish tradition always used a family name in historical documents and genealogies. I have chosen to use his Syrian name.

There are many questions I tried to answer through the medium of historical fiction. What was his life like before he discovered he had the most dreaded disease of all time—leprosy? What was the name of the servant girl who became the means of his salvation? What made him immerse himself the seventh time when nothing had happened the other six times he plunged beneath the muddy Jordan River? What happened on his journeys to and from the city of Samaria? Was he still a general when he returned healed and in perfect health? What did he do with the two bushels of soil taken from Elisha's garden when he returned to Damascus? And there were so many other questions whose answers I have tried to resolve in this novel.

It is hoped the reader will not only read chapter five in Second Kings where the focus is on Naaman himself, but also the chapters before and after the event to understand the context. The goal of the book is of course to uplift, inspire and encourage the reader to live a life that dares to believe. Above all, may it bring glory and honor to the Lord for His faithfulness to not only his people Israel, but to the whole world.

TABLE OF CONTENTS

CHAPTER ONE

DAMASCUS

The dust burned Naaman's eyes. Rubbing them only made matters worse. "We'll stop up ahead by that stream," he commanded his aide. The leader of the Syrian army and friend of the king had grown tired of driving. The constant jarring of the chariot wheels over stones and holes in the road proved hard on his back. He preferred riding horseback and decided at this break he would make the change.

Captain Ishme rode back to tell the rest of the company they were stopping. One of his men complained. "Come on, Sir, we're anxious to get home."

"That's enough, Nimar. Do as you're told," Ishme said. The soldier grumbled something, but Ishme had already turned his horse around and headed back to the front of the column.

Naaman reined in his team of horses and his groom unhitched them so they could drink from the stream and graze. Removing his leather breastplate and sandals, he waded into the water. His warriors did the same, relieved to feel something cool on their bare feet.

"Make sure the detail in charge of the prisoners is on alert," Naaman said.

Ishme, was washing the dust from his face. "There you go insulting me again, my Lord," Ishme grumbled. "Trust me to do my job." With the sound of a hammer on soft wood, an arrow struck him in the shoulder, knocking him over.

"Ambush!" Naaman shouted. His men scattered and archers rushed forward to surround their commander. "Up there," he yelled, pointing to a tall sycamore. Dozens of arrows flew into the branches of the tree, knocking their attackers to the ground.

"Death to all Syrian dogs," one of the enemy cried out before a soldier ended his life.

Naaman rushed to Ishme's side. The arrow had pierced his left shoulder. He handed his friend the leather handle of his dagger. "Bite on this brother," he said. As the officer did so, the general quickly broke off the arrow, leaving a few inches sticking out. "Call the healer," he ordered. The physician had already headed for the general's position.

"Start a fire," the elderly man ordered. He selected the knife he would need and sterilized the blade in the fire. After giving Ishme several cups of wine, he began the painful process of cutting out the arrowhead.

"A curse of the gods on all Israelites," Naaman yelled. "I want those assassin's bodies burned!"

Ropes cut into Joseph's wrists. He and the other prisoners that included two women and his friend, Asher, were tied to a rope pulled by a horse soldier. The Syrians had taken them captive during a raid into Israelite territory. Suddenly the rope went slack and the prisoners were relieved the soldiers were stopping.

One of their captors approached. "Drink now and bread will be brought for you." He turned to his comrade and began speaking Hurrian, a Mitanni dialect.

Joseph understood every word. He whispered a translation to his friends. "We'll be treated well. Apparently these soldiers belong to a general of the king of Syria. They said some of us would be assigned to their commander's household."

"Servants," Asher spit on the ground. "We're free people and now we must serve our enemies?"

"True enough, Brother," Joseph said. He turned toward the two young women who were from the same village, and his heart went out to them.

"I'm sorry for your parents, Meira," he stammered. When he saw the sadness in her eyes, he regretted his words. The soldiers had attacked their village in plain daylight, cutting down everyone in their path. Asher and Joseph had tried to defend their farms, but pitchforks were no match for Syrian swords.

"May their names be remembered," Meira prayed.

"Let it be so," the other three recited.

As they drank from a small stream, Joseph told the two women what else he had learned. "You will not to be harmed," he said. "The one who brought us the bread said you two will be given to the general's wife as her personal servants."

Deborah's face colored with anger. "Slaves you mean," she hissed. "To be a slave is a dishonor."

Meira shook her head. "Perhaps the Lord has a purpose in all this."

Deborah only grumbled. "These pagans don't even know the Lord, Meira. What purpose could our God have in making us slaves?"

Meira wouldn't be intimidated. "From what Joseph said, it sounds like we'll be servants, not slaves. If so, we must be the best servants we can be."

Asher growled, "It's beyond reason for anyone to think as you do. Doesn't the killing of your family mean anything?" Joseph regretted his words again, seeing how they cut into the young woman's heart.

Meira had to look away, her eyes filling with tears.

The army physician sent his servant to treat the prisoner's wounds when they stopped. He helped wash and then smoothed ointment on the cuts and rope burns.

"We're grateful," Meira said. "Tell the healer what we said."

The man didn't reply, but returned to his master's wagon up ahead.

Deborah muttered, "I don't know why you are so polite, Meira. They're the enemy."

"I'm only trying to make our lives easier. We'll have to live with them, won't we?"

Joseph frowned. "Who cares anyway? Our lives are over. We have nothing to live for."

"Get back in line," a guard shouted in Aramaic. Two soldiers tied them once more to the line and the prisoners hurried into position so the lead horse wouldn't jerk them along. The regiment and their prisoners were heading for Damascus, another two days away.

In General Naman's villa in the capital city of Damascus, Lady Adorina stood facing the two women prisoners. "How are you called?" She asked the Israelite women in Aramaic, the ancient language of the two countries. Naaman's wife wore a robe made of the finest linen dyed a deep green, and a golden necklace circled her neck.

"I am Meira, my Lady," the youngest replied.

Adorina looked at the other girl. "And you?"

"Deborah," the young woman said. She didn't use the polite title for her mistress. Lady Adorina did not make it an issue.

"My husband has assigned you to our household and Nirar the house steward, will show you what to do. To serve in this house is an honor."

"To be a slave anywhere is to be a dog," Deborah grumbled.

The steward, who had been standing behind them, rushed forward and grabbed Deborah by the arm. Before she could say anything, he dragged her toward the back garden. He had picked up a bamboo whip hanging near the entrance and raised it to strike the young woman.

"Nirar," Adorina called. "These servants are not to be mistreated. We can forgive her remarks. They're only natural." Turning to the two women she said, "Follow me." With the wave of her hand, she dismissed Nirar. She led the women through the back garden and stopped in front of the servant's quarters.

"This will be your room," she said. Looking directly at Deborah she added, "I will not tolerate brutality in this house. Be careful what you say before the Master, however. He will not be as understanding."

"Yes Mistress," Meira replied. She bowed her head with respect. The two Israelites entered their room and Deborah expressed her anger toward her friend by being silent. Meira lay down on her small cot and stretched out. She knew better than say anything, so she closed her eyes and the two fell into an exhausted sleep.

The next morning, the steward came for them and led them to the kitchen.

"Ah there you are," Lady Adorina said. You will not be cooking any meals, but when Kora has prepared the food, you'll serve it." The mistress of the house stood at the doorway and smiled as Kora frowned at the two women.

"Sit here and watch how things are done," the cook ordered. When she finished preparing the plates, she motioned for Meira to come forward. "The food is ready. Get along with you." Turning to Deborah, she said, "You stay here and help me clean up."

Lady Adorina met Meira in the hallway. "Take the master's tray to the dining room. Remember, not to speak unless spoken to. Above all, do not look him in the eye. Do you understand?"

Meira smiled. "Yes, Mistress."

Walking slowly down the polished stone hall, Meira tried to find the dining room. When she saw the general sitting at a long table, she became nervous. He looked up for a fleeting instant as the young woman entered and placed the tray in front of him.

Looking up, the nobleman asked, "Where's my pomegranate juice?"

Meira forgot what she had been told and looked directly at her new master with a smile. "I'll go get some at once, my Lord," she said. She didn't wait for his permission to speak or leave. When she returned with the juice, she placed it in front of him and stood off to the side as instructed.

"What is your name?" Naaman asked.

"Meira, my Lord, and it is an honor to serve you." Looking at him closely for the first time she liked what she saw. He had a strong face with a bronze complexion and a short well-trimmed beard. She liked his curly golden hair and guessed him to be in his late twenties or early thirties.

"Come here," the Syrian commanded, and Meira obeyed. "You're not afraid of me, are you?"

"Yes and no, noble one," she said. "I fear you as the general who destroyed my village, but not as the nobleman who has been kind enough to place me here in his home."

The warrior laughed and put down his juice. "By the gods! That is an excellent answer." He looked at her more closely. "Do you know who I am?"

"You are the king's Right Hand, General Naaman. Everyone knows you. At least that's what your steward told us."

Naaman laughed again. "Bring me Nirar," he ordered. Meira did so, and when the steward came into the room the general said, "This servant is to be the only one to bring me my meals. She makes me laugh. Is that clear?"

Nirar glanced at the new servant and bowed to his master. "Yes, my Lord General."

When the morning meal was over, and the dishes cleaned and put away, the two Israelite companions had a few moments by themselves in the garden.

"I like the general," Meira said matter-of-factly.

Her companion snapped, "How can you like such a butcher?"

Meira quickly changed the subject. "At least we have a beautiful room and real feather mattresses." Suddenly Deborah began to weep and Meira put an arm around her.

"Oh Meira," her friend sobbed, "this *is* a beautiful place, but I hate them for what they did. I cannot forgive them." She wiped the tears from her face and stood. Walking over to a small reflecting pool, she sat on the edge and ran her fingers along the top of the water. Pink water lilies floated on the surface and she touched the soft luxurious petals.

Meira followed and sat down next to her. "We're different, Debra," she whispered. "My father, may his name be remembered, always taught me not to dwell on the bad, only on the good. I'm as sad over the loss of our families as you. But there is nothing we can do to change that." She paused and her eyes followed a golden fish swimming among the lilies.

Deborah looked at her with the beginning of a smile. "Well, the Mistress seems to be a gentle person. One of the kitchen girls told me she comes from a very noble family who opposed her marriage to the general. Now she feels cursed by their gods because she cannot have children."

"Oh?" Meira responded. "A sad time for her, or any woman."

"Yes. I promise to try to be helpful and understanding toward her." She paused and said, "The cook told me the two women we are replacing were allowed to return to their villages. The staff really liked them and said they were good workers. I don't think she likes us. We'll have a lot to learn."

"I agree," Meira said. The two young women stood and headed back to the kitchen.

The next day, Naaman looked up as Meira served his morning meal. He smiled at her, knowing it put her at ease. She asked him if she might speak.

"Of course, Meira. What is it?"

"Deborah and I have observed the sadness on our mistress's face, Master, and she has told us the reason." The general frowned but she hurriedly continued. "I just wanted your permission to pray to my God to help her, my Lord."

Naaman stood and moved away from the table. "Servants do not meddle in the affairs of their masters, young lady." Meira bowed her head and averted her eyes. He continued, "However, what you offer to do is a kind gesture. I will allow it providing it will be kept as a private matter."

Meira looked at him with a smile. She said, "Of course, Master. We have faith that our God will hear our prayers. Thank you." She bowed her head again politely. "Can I bring you anything else Lord General?" When he shook his head, she left the room.

"Ah, you've finished, Husband," his wife said entering the dining room.

"Yes my Morning Star," he said. He walked over and put his arms around her. "Sit with me a moment." They walked to a cushioned divan at the edge of the veranda and sat down. "Meira has just asked me a touching question."

Adorina raised her eyebrows. "Oh? She should not have spoken to you, my Lord. I'll discuss this with her."

"No, Dorina, listen. She only wanted to ask me if she could pray to her god about us. She wants to ask him to give us a child."

Adorina's eyes misted over and she looked away.

He took her hand and held it for a moment. "I told her it would be a kind thing to do. Isn't it amazing that after everything I've done to her, she now wants to pray for us?"

"And what did you say, Naaman?"

"I gave my consent, providing she keeps it to herself. Did I do right?"

She squeezed his hand. "I do so want to give you a son, Naaman. If their god can do so, then who am I to object?"

"Good," her husband declared, kissing her on the cheek. "I've been summoned by the king. He's sending me on another mission." They embraced, and then he went to put on his dress uniform.

Naaman found King Hadadezer standing on the palace veranda overlooking Damascus. The large city, built on a plateau, faced the beautiful Abana River flowing through it on two sides. Its two streams flowed around each side of the city. East of the city another river, the Pharpar, meandered through a marshy lake, blessing the inhabitants with an abundance of water. The sun caught the ripples on the water making the king smile. A portly man in his late thirties, Hadadezer still carried himself as a soldier.

Naaman saluted the king with his right fist extended. "Majesty."

The king turned around. "Ah, Naaman. Come, we have much to discuss." The general followed him down the hallway to the king's council chamber. The only people around were the guards on duty who stood outside the room as the two men entered.   Captain Duzi, head of the royal guards saluted them and stood at attention inside the room. His duty called for him to protect the king at all times but Hadadezer said, "You are dismissed, good friend. Naaman will not harm me."

"It is against regulations, Majesty," the captain protested. But when he saw the king's frown, he simply shrugged his shoulders, saluted again, and left the room.

After a few moments of polite talk about wives and family, the king pulled out another chair and put his feet up.

"I want you to keep up the raids against Israel," he insisted. "I want to keep King Jehoram off balance. And even though there's no immediate threat to the State, you should remain here in Damascus. Use your regiment commanders to carry out the raids."

Naaman nodded. "As you command, Majesty. Our booty has not been worth much—only a few slaves and some cattle. Their harvest is done."

"Well that will still leave even less for them," Hadadezer growled. "I've never forgiven King Jehoram for not joining the alliance of twelve kings when we tried to fight off Shalmaneser. Never." He referred to the great battle at Qarqar and the battle at the Orontes River. "At least we kept them from further invasion."

Naaman laughed. "Thanks to the gods. I've got a scar here somewhere from that day."

The king laughed with him. "As do I. We both should have died in that battle."

"That's the truth, my Lord," Naaman sighed.

The king leaned toward him and said quietly, "I have reason to believe our friend Duzi is involved in a plot to kill me!"

Naaman's jaw dropped in disbelief. "What?"

CHAPTER TWO

A TIME OF HOPE

"It can't be true, Majesty!" Naaman exclaimed.

"I know," Hadadezer said. "That's how I felt when I learned of it. He's my cousin for Dagan's sake." The king anticipated Naaman's next question. "My steward Samula discovered the plot quite by accident." The king stood and walked slowly around the room as he talked. "He happened to be in here," he said, pointing to a small alcove where the servants stored cups and wine for the king's councils. "He stood there drying my cup when several guards burst into what they thought to be an empty room. Samula crouched down, not wanting to be accused of spying, and remained silent."

Naaman shifted on his chair, listening intently.

"It was Duzi with two of his sergeants," the king continued. "Samula heard the captain say that they had to bide their time. They'd strike when his cousin was alone. The queen would be leaving for a visit to her family. It would be the perfect time to kill him."

The king stopped pacing and turned toward his friend. "I don't want to believe it, brother. I've known Duzi my whole life, but he is an ambitious man. I also trust my steward, as I do you, so we must take this seriously. Queen Atalia left yesterday, Naaman. I want you to bring your personal guard here to the palace without Duzi knowing."

Naaman stood and walked toward the door. He yanked it open quickly, worried that someone might be listening, but found no one.

"Let me think, Majesty," he said. He began scratching his head. "There are too many servants around during the day. Courtiers are always coming and going, so Duzi will have to attack at night when you're asleep. Who stays in the palace with you, my Lord?"

Hadadezer stopped pacing, giving the question some thought. "Samula, my steward is close by in case I need him. Of course there are also the two guards outside the door as you know."

"Yes, and Duzi will make sure *his* sergeants replace them when he makes his move," Namaan growled. "I'll stay here tonight, Majesty, but no one must know. I would advise you not to be alone today, even for a moment. Keep a servant or councilor near you on whatever pretext, but keep people nearby. I'll go and work out a plan and be back before nightfall."

The king shook his head. "I can't believe Duzi would do this." Then, he put his hand on Naaman's shoulder. "I can't give you any higher reward than what you've already achieved, brother—only my everlasting gratitude."

"We've known each other since we were boys, 'Dezer. To serve you is my greatest honor. You know that. We must make sure these men are intercepted and killed."

"Make it so. The gods go with you."

His friend bowed his head for an instant, then left the chamber.

The king followed and saw one of his counselors walking past. "Lord Gindibu, greetings, my friend."

The startled old man turned and smiled at the king.

"Let's discuss that land you wanted last week. Come out on my veranda where it's cool and we'll talk."

"What?" Captain Ishme said indignantly. "I don't believe it," Naaman's aide protested when Naaman told him of Duzi's plot. Captain Ishme had been the general's right hand for more than five years, fighting beside him in two wars. His commander treated him as a trusted friend.

"This is what we have to do tonight," Naaman began. "I will enter the king's bedchamber somehow and take his place. You'll move him into the adjoining queen's room with four of our best men. You and I will hide in the king's chamber, and when Duzi strikes, we'll grab him."

"All right, the younger warrior said. " It's a good plan, but full of holes."

"Oh? How so?" Naaman retorted.

Ishme scrunched his eyebrows. "Well, first of all, General, how do we get into the palace without being seen?"

Naaman grinned. "I've already thought of that. It won't be easy, but you know the fountain that's being repaired at the back of the king's garden?" Ishme nodded.

"Well, your men will replace them at midday and give the workmen the rest of the day off. Make sure to give them enough beer money. As the afternoon progresses your men will disappear into the garden and remain hidden until the sun sets. The door to the king's bedchamber opens out onto the garden. When all is clear, I'll let you in."

"All right," Ishme said. "However, the palace staff have seen the masons working on the wall. They'll know my men don't belong there."

Naaman frowned. "It's not a *perfect* plan, Captain. We'll have to leave a lot of this to the gods. Agreed?"

Ishme still shook his head stubbornly. "What if Duzi and his two sergeants decide to kill the king? Can you and I handle three of them?"

"They won't know what hit them," Naaman said. He snapped his fingers, making his friend laugh.

"Good. I'll get our men ready. How will you get back in without being seen, General?" Ishme asked.

"I have my ways. Now be gone."

Later that night, a knock on the door of the king's bedchamber sent Naaman into hiding behind the curtains.

"Are you all right, Majesty?" Captain Duzi asked.

The king opened the door just enough to speak to him. Duzi came every night at the same time to check on their majesties before they retired. "Yes, I'm fine, Captain. Good night."

"Good night. Rest well, Great King," Duzi answered. The king shut the door.

Through the peephole Naaman watched as Duzi nodded to his co-conspirators standing at attention outside the door.

"He's walking back to his post in the hallway," Naaman whispered. "He'll probably wait until the middle of the night."

Ishme entered through the door connecting the queen's bedchamber, asking the king to return with him.

Naaman slipped into the king's bed, keeping his shortsword ready for an attack. The half moon had set and darkness filled the king's chamber. Ishme came back and hid behind the curtains covering the door to the garden. He stood as rigid as an iron rod, not daring to breathe. For both warriors, time passed very slowly.

The only sound heard for most of the night, came from an owl screeching in the garden. Abruptly, the door opened and three shadowy figures moved toward the bed. Naaman's worst scenario began to play out. *Three* attackers came into the room instead of two. Naaman leapt from the bed and thrust his sword into the startled assassin closest to him. Ishme threw back the curtain and stabbed another attacker in the back. As the fatally injured man cried out, Naaman struck out at the remaining assassin. Iron met iron as their weapons struck, and Ishme rushed to Naaman's side.

"You'll pay for this, Duzi," Naaman shouted.

"Not if you die first," the guardsman shouted back.

"Take him alive, Ishme," Naaman ordered. They fought hand-to-hand, moving about the room, each trying to gain an advantage

King Hadadezer, eager to see the fight, rushed into the chamber with his sword. One of Naaman's men brought a torch, throwing light on the fighters. Duzi seized the sudden distraction and slashed out at Naaman, knocking the general to the floor. Naaman's cry of pain brought the soldiers from the other room, who quickly overpowered the assassin.

Grabbing the torch, the king walked toward Duzi and shouted, "Let me see the face of the traitor." Stomping his foot down on the neck of his attacker, he spit on him. "May the gods of darkness take your soul, Cousin. Your eyes will not see another day."

"Over here, Majesty!" Ishme called to the king. Hadadezer turned and saw why the officer had called him. There was a deep bloody gash in Naaman's side, and blood gushed from it.

"Call the physician," the king shouted. "Tear that sheet and wrap it tightly around the wound. Hurry."

Ishme did so, putting pressure on the cut. His men helped Naaman stand but he refused to lie down again on the king's bed.

"Better he cut me than you, Great King," Naaman said.

"I owe you my life, brother," the king answered. "Gods, where *is* that surgeon?" he yelled at the top of his voice. "Get these bodies out of here," he ordered. Ishme's men had already restrained and gagged Duzi.

A disheveled healer rushed into the room with his medicine bag and examined the general's wound. "Get him to that table!" the man ordered, "with your permission, Majesty."

"Carry on," Hadadezer said.

"Remove his tunic, and bring me a basin of water—quickly," the healer said. When it arrived, he ordered, "Keep the pressure on the wound while I cleanse all around it." Turning to Naaman he said, "Bite on this, my Lord while I sew it up." He handed the general a small wooden baton to bite down on against the pain.

"No need," Naaman replied. "Just get on with it."

"Spoken like so many foolish soldiers," the physician said. He put down the baton. "Always trying to show how brave you are." He carefully sewed shut the six-inch gash with catgut. The king and Ishme stepped away a short distance, so Naaman could cry out without embarrassment.

"Take your men, Captain," the king said, "and lock up Duzi. Keep a close guard. I want to personally be there to end his life."

The captain saluted with his fist and arm straight out as his men led the prisoner away.

Lord Ninurta, the physician, approached the king. "The general should stay in the palace, Majesty. The danger of infection is always the greatest risk in these injuries, as you know. I'll stay and keep an eye on him."

"Let me go home, Majesty," Naaman said. "Send Ninurta with me."

The king grinned. "I'm not used to having people tell me what to do, General. My steward will help you move into my son's old room. You'll stay with us until I say you can leave."

Naaman smiled. "Very well, as you command, Majesty."

"Good, now settle down."

The sun was coming up and servants were beginning to arrive at their posts. The king told his steward what to do and within a short time evidence of Naaman's injury had disappeared. Naaman had been carried to the other bedchamber and even though sedated, he could still hear the physician talking.

"He'll sleep soon, Majesty," Naaman heard Ninurta say. "I gave him a sedative in the wine. Let's pray there will be no fever."

"Even so, my Lord. I am grateful for your care of my friend. See that he stays alive."

"I'll rest now," Hadadezer told the servants. "I am not to be disturbed."

Naaman imagined the king stretching out on a clean bed and falling asleep. .

"It's about time you woke up," Naaman grumbled. The king had entered the spare bedroom, stretching his arms. Naaman's wife had been sitting in a chair beside him and he held her hand, watching her sleep. She suddenly awoke and saw the king. Prostrating herself before him, she awaited his pleasure.

"Adorina," the king whispered. "Oh my Lady, please stand. As you can see your husband has been well cared for." Realizing he had not finished dressing he added, "You must excuse me," and he turned and left the bedchamber.

Naaman smiled. "Where's Ishme?"

"Outside in the hall, Husband," she said. She went and opened the door inviting their friend in.

Ishme smiled. "So the gods let you live, did they?"

The king returned looking refreshed, and had put on a different robe. Adorina started to make obeisance again, and Ishme knelt, but he gestured for them to be seated.

"Forgive me, Great One," Adorina said. "Word reached me of the attempt on your life. They said Naaman was wounded and I just had to come. Forgive me."

"No, be at ease dear Lady," the king replied. "Your husband has been slightly injured when he saved me again. It is a debt I cannot repay. I owe him my life." He went on to tell her of her husband's clever trap and of their struggle.

Lord Ninurta heard voices in his patient's room and entered. Checking his patient he said, "He has no fever, Majesty. That is a good sign."

"Indeed," Hadadezer said. "We'll offer a sacrifice to Rimmon this very day"

"Make it so," Naaman replied. "You must let me go home, Majesty."

The king looked at the physician who reluctantly nodded in agreement.

"Everyone is saying how you escaped, Majesty," Adorina told him. "The people are happy for you."

"Then I shall personally drive my general to his home," Hadadezer said. "Prepare my horse and a wagon for the wounded," he ordered. The steward ran out to the guards with the king's command.

A short time later, the people of Damascus crowded the boulevard to cheer the king and his commander.

Naaman, lying in the wagon with his wife at his side, groaned every time the driver drove over a rough spot. "Why are we stopping here?" he protested.

"His majesty is going into the temple to sacrifice a bull in thanksgiving to Rimmon, Husband," Adorina explained. "He's grateful his life and the life of his friend have been spared."

A short time later, the king came out of the sacred building and the people clapped and shouted his name. Climbing back on his horse he rode alongside Naaman through the city and out the city gates. Naaman's house was but a short distance up in the hills where several of the king's advisors lived. A large crowd had gathered in front of the general's villa. Hadadezer walked up the steps and turned around to face his people.

"Dear friends," he said in a loud voice. "Our god, Rimmon, has protected us through the courage of our general. Pray for his complete recovery." The crowd clapped again and began to sing songs of joy. Once inside the house, however, the king refused any wine or sweet cakes. "You are tired, Naaman," he said, genuinely concerned for his friend's health. "Allow me to lead the crowd away so you can have peace and quiet." Naaman's servants helped him to his bedchamber as the king said farewell to Adorina.

Patting her hand he said, "Take care of him, my Lady."

"We women have seen our men wounded before, Great King. Your Queen will be beside herself when she finds out what nearly happened. May the gods bless you for your kindness."

Outside, the people continued to applaud the king, but he had his soldiers move the crowd slowly back towards the city.

Inside their chamber, Adorina smiled at Naaman who had collapsed on the bed, exhausted. His body needed time to recuperate.

The next day, the servants helped him out into the garden. He reclined on a divan brought out for him. Meira and Deborah stayed with him in case he needed anything.

Ignoring him completely, Meira said, "He's such a brave man, Mistress. To offer his life in place of the king takes a strong and daring man."

Naaman frowned. "I'm right here, Meira. Don't speak as if I'm unconscious."

"You are brave like David of old," Deborah remarked. She said it wistfully, remembering her people's history.

Adorina said, "Tell us about this David."

Meira told them about the young Hebrew king who fought a giant and defeated the Philistine enemy.

"He won, my Lady, because our God blessed him," Deborah said.

"With your permission, General. We will pray to our God to heal you."

Naaman shook his head. "No, my god Rimmon will help me."

Lady Adorina spoke up. "You have our permission to pray for him. He needs everyone's prayers, and we thank you for them."

Naaman only mumbled something and closed his eyes.

Within two weeks Naaman felt revitalized by the forced rest and wanted to return to the palace. He had also been showing an unexpected but gentle affection toward his wife, delighting her.

One evening after they had made love carefully, but with great passion. Adorina spoke just above a whisper. "You are behaving as you did when we were first married, Husband."

Naaman grinned. "And you are like a sweet invigorating wine, Dearest One. I can't drink enough." She laughed, and he loved the way she laughed. The sound of it had attracted him to her when they first met years ago. The next day, to his regret, she chased him out of the house, encouraging him to go back to work.

A short time later in the garden, Lady Adorina seemed especially radiant and happy. Meira and Deborah noticed it immediately. When she went into the house at mid-morning, Meira said, "They really do love each other, don't they."

"They're behaving like newlyweds. Such a thing," her friend replied. "I wish I could meet such a man."

"And I," her companion whispered. "If only the Lord would give them a child."

Several weeks later, Lady Adorina called them into her chamber and had them sit down beside her dressing table. "Are you still praying to your god on our behalf?"

"Yes, Mistress," Meira answered. "Have we done wrong?"

Adorina laughed gently. "You may have done something very *right*. I have missed my cycle and the physician tells me I could be with child. He'll know better in a month."

"Ah," Meira exclaimed. "May the Lord be praised." She jumped up with excitement. "Oh it must be true. Isn't that wonderful, Debra?"

"Yes, my Lady. We are happy for you and our Master." Deborah surprised herself when the words rushed out, because she realized she really meant it.

A month later, Naaman's villa became a place of serious confinement for the expectant mother.

"Please, Husband," Adorina implored one afternoon as Meira made up her bed. "Must my every meal be scrutinized and specially prepared?"

Naaman smiled. "The servants mean well, Dorina. I'll tell them to stop being so demanding. They're only doing what they think is best for you and the baby."

Meira noticed that Naaman couldn't help but spoil her and cater to her every wish.

The highlight of her time of confinement came when Queen Atalia arrived to spend time with her. Not only did Adorina consider it a great honor, but she enjoyed the woman's company.

Later, Adorina told her servants, "These months have seemed to last forever for Naaman. I insisted he and the king go hunting. I wanted him to take his mind off my condition."

"That is understandable Mistress," Meira replied. "Men are useless at these times."

Finally, in her ninth month—in the middle of the day—they called the midwives. Lady Adorina had gone into labor.

"I've sent the men to the garden," Meira told the household. "Waiting, that's all men can do."

Naaman and Ishme, confined to the garden, drank wine and waited impatiently. Once, when Meira came running by, Naaman called to her.

"When you prayed to your god, Meira, what did you pray for? A girl or a boy?"

Meira giggled. "Why a boy of course, Master. I know it will be a boy." Laughing happily again, she headed back into the house, but overheard the men talking.

"Let's hope she is also a Seer," Captain Ishme exclaimed. "A general *should* have a son!"

"I pray you're right," Naaman said.

Meira saw him grin.

⊕

Baby Ashur-Rash-Ishi didn't enter this world for another whole day, but at midnight his cry echoed throughout the villa. The two men, who had fallen asleep, suddenly jerked awake at the sound. Laughing triumphantly they patted each other on the back. A few minutes later, the head midwife called for him, and Naaman entered the large front room of the house. She handed him a small, well-wrapped baby.

"You have a son, General," she announced. "May the gods be praised."

He looked down at the baby's wrinkled face, and tears filled his eyes. Joy almost burst his heart. "And my dear wife? Is she all right?"

"She is doing well, General. While the labor lasted long, she is fine. Nothing happened out of the ordinary," the old woman said. "But she needs her rest for now,"

He nodded, showed his son to Ishme, then, gave the baby back to the midwife. He looked in on Adorina sleeping soundly. As he walked through the house, his servants congratulated him. Out in the garden, he thanked Ishme for watching with him. Meira anticipated her master's wish and brought them some more wine.

When she served them, Naaman said, "Not only has your god blessed us with a child, Meira, he has given me a son. I owe you and Deborah a great deal and I pay my debts. Come and see me at mid-morning after I've had a chance to speak to my wife."

"Yes, Master. We too must thank our God. It is He who is to be praised."

"Then let it be so," the general said.

The next day, when Adorina awoke and had nursed her son, she and her husband had a long talk. Afterward, he called for the two Hebrew women and had them sit down.

"Because you prayed for us, and because your god answered your prayers, my family has been blessed. Therefore my wife and I have decided to set you free and let you return to your homeland."

"Oh," Deborah cried out falling onto her knees. "Our freedom! O Master may the Lord God of Israel bless you for what you are doing. We are free, Meira."

"Yes," her friend said. "We are grateful, Master. We did not hope for such a gift."

Naaman smiled. "Tomorrow you can begin packing. I'll send Captain Ishme to accompany you to the border. I must confess we'll miss you both. You have become a part of our family."

"Thank you, General," Meira answered. "Our God will bless you for this." The young servants stood and hurried to their room. Stretching out on their beds, they spoke excitedly about what had just happened. Meira suddenly blurted out, "I'm not going."

"What?" Deborah exclaimed, sitting up on her bed. "Are you serious, Meira?"

"Yes. I have no one back home, and I like serving these people. They are kind and generous to us. I choose to stay here. The captain will take you home, sister, but don't make me go with you."

"But you were the one who told me the Lord would release us one day and we *would* go home. That's now happened. It would be wrong to refuse God's gift."

"Maybe, Debra. But I feel the Lord wants me here. Please be happy for me."

Deborah turned toward her. "Be happy for me too, sister. I'll miss you."

Meira said, "And I you. May the Lord go with you." As they lay back on their straw mattresses, Meira's heart raced with excitement. Tomorrow their lives would change again and only their God knew what would happen.

CHAPTER THREE

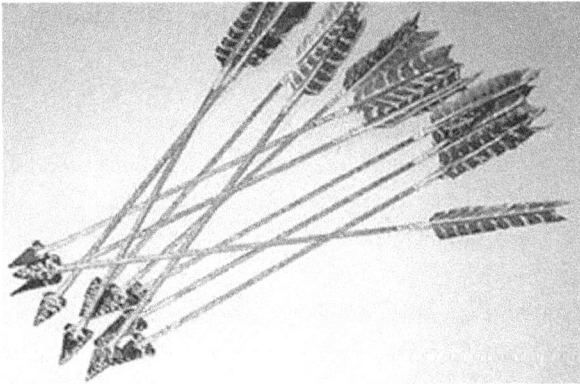

ARROW'S DANGER

Two years passed and Meira watched little Ashur grow by leaps and bounds. He became the sun around which the family revolved. But at the end of that year a sister joined him, and the boy had to learn to share the attention. Ashur, now almost three, followed Meira around like a devoted puppy. He could speak quite well and he pestered her with endless questions.

"Why are you doing that?" he asked.

"Because your father likes these masks polished, my Lord," Meira explained. "Your father often brings home beautiful things he's found in his enemies' villages."

"Why?" the boy asked.

She laughed. "To make little boys ask me questions."

"I'm not little," Ashur pouted. "Mother says I'm very big."

"Yes, you are big, young Lord, but not as big as your father."

"I will be one day," he shot back.

"You won't be if you don't finish your lesson, my Lord," Meira reminded him. A sudden noise outside caught the boy's attention.

"It's Ishme," he shouted. "He's come in his chariot," and before Meira could stop him Ashur ran out the front door. She rushed after him but he quickly jumped up into Captain Ishme's arms.

"Uncle! Let me ride with you!"

The officer smiled at Meira. "All right, just once around the circle,"

She watched as Ishme tied a leather restraint around the small boy and attached it to the front of the chariot. Flicking the reins, the two of them rode slowly around the circle in front of the villa. Ishme did it twice, and then brought his horse to a stop.

Helping the boy down, Meira laughed as the captain threw him up over his shoulders and marched into the house. Walking through the villa and into the garden he found Lady Adorina resting with her newborn. Baby Atalia cooed, smiling at her mother. They had received royal permission to name the child in honor of the queen and her majesty often came by for a visit.

Meira said to Ishme, "Ashur loves his baby sister and enjoys being around her now."

"I knew he would come around," the captain said.

Bowing his head to Lady Adorina he said, "The general is going to be late, my Lady."

Meira saw her mistress's look of disappointment and frowned at him.

Ishme was quick to add, "His Majesty called a council meeting for late this afternoon and they must all attend. He wanted you to know."

"Thank you Captain," Adorina sighed. "You'd think I'd be used to it by now. Won't you have some refreshment before going back?"

Meira motioned for him to accept. "With pleasure, thank you," he replied.

Adorina suggested he be seated in the shade near her. Little Ashur sat down next to him, mimicking his every move.

Meira quickly left and returned from the kitchen with a tray. "I've brought some cooled wine and pastries, my Lady," Meira said. "There's also some fruit juice for Master Ashur." She then took her place on a bench near her mistress.

As they sipped their drinks, Adorina looked at him seriously. "What could be so important to convene the council?"

Ishme set his cup down. "King Joram of Israel has sent a raiding party across the border again. The general wants the council to approve reprisals by the army." He paused and took a bite out of his small cake. "It's an endless conflict, I'm afraid."

Meira wanted to defend her country's actions, but held her tongue.

"I'm going to be a soldier when I'm big enough," Ashur declared, his mouth full of sweet crumbs.

"If you eat too many sugar cakes, my son," Adorina said, "you'll be too big and fat to fight anyone." The three adults chuckled, but Ashur took exception.

"Then you must feed me only what will make me grow taller, Mother," he said.

Adorina laughed again. "Good! Did you hear that Meira. This means he will eat all of his vegetables from now on. That'll make him grow tall and strong."

"She's right, Ashur," Ishme laughed. "But forgive me, Little General, I must be going." Standing, he nodded to Adorina, taking Ashur by the hand back to his chariot. Meira smiled as she watched the young boy salute like a soldier, his little fist and arm straight out. Ishme laughed, and returned the salute as he drove off.

A week later, several companies of the Syrian army patrolled their border with Israel, looking for a fight. One night, Naaman stretched out on his blanket and let out a long sigh. "I love it out here," he breathed. "The fresh air, the campfires, yes, even the bad food."

"Don't you miss Adorina and your children, my Lord?" Ishme mumbled.

"Of course. Don't *you* miss women?" He grinned at his bachelor aide, notorious for his many encounters with women.

"Yes my Lord, but I agree with you. It's good to get away for a while. It makes them that much more attractive when we return home."

Naaman nodded in agreement. As the fire died down the general and his men fell asleep, leaving the night watch on the alert.

In the morning, they bathed in the small river near camp. The cold water felt invigorating, but as Naaman washed, he suddenly winced in pain. The water had irritated a sore on his left forearm. He looked at it closely but afterwards, didn't think more about it. As a soldier, scrapes and cuts were not unusual, but this spot would not heal. After drying off, he tore a piece of cloth from his sleeve and wrapped it around the sore.

Ishme saw the small bandage. "Something bite you in the night, General?"

"It's nothing. Who's riding with me today?"

"Ilani and Kala, my Lord. I'll take Samsi and Kapu."

As he dressed, Naaman asked, "Does Kala ever shut up?"

His friend laughed. "Tell him he'll have to do the cooking, General. That'll silence him."

Naaman chuckled, remembering the young soldier's dislike of preparing food.

As they saddled their horses, Ishme looked across the field at some buildings. "We are near the village where I brought your servant Deborah three years ago."

"Oh?" Naaman said. "Adorina and I were glad she made it home safely."

The captain mounted his horse, as did the general. "Well she didn't live here, but she knew a family in the village. We waited until dark and I walked with her as far as I dared go myself. She thanked me and went up to the door of the house. I could see the surprise of the people as they recognized her, and could hear the laughter and clapping as they took her inside." He paused a moment. "I would rather not cause any trouble to that village, General, with your permission."

"Agreed. My wife loved Deborah, so to honor both of them, we'll leave them alone, and ride farther east."

"Mount up," Ishme ordered their men and when ready, Naaman led them toward the mountains of Lebanon. On the road, villagers ran from them in fear for their lives, but the Syrians didn't give pursuit. Just being there accomplished what the soldiers wanted.

However, as they approached the Kitani River and were about to cross, arrows rained down on them. "Cover," Ishme shouted, "They're in those boulders up ahead."

Naaman dismounted and crouched down as Ilani and Kapu took aim at the snipers. Other warriors rushed to the far side and joined them. Something struck Naaman in the arm and he doubled over in pain. The ambush didn't last long and the Israelites were quickly destroyed. But when Ishme turned toward the general, he saw Naaman kneeling beside his mount with an arrow through his upper arm.

He ran to his side. "General," he shouted.

"Break off the ends," Naaman ordered. "But don't pull it through."

Ishme gritted his teeth and broke off the two ends of the weapon. He then wrapped the wound and broken stumps with strips of cloth torn from his own tunic. The rest of the patrol rushed to their commander and huddled around.

"I'll be fine once the healer removes the shaft," he told them. Naaman knew it to be so. He had seen it many times.

"Let's mount up again," Ishme commanded, "we'll head back to Damascus."

"This won't be the last ambush you know," Naaman said. "Remember three years ago?"

Ishme nodded, frowning. "I guess this time it happened to be your turn, General."

"I'm only concerned this might weaken my right arm—my fighting arm."

They rode all afternoon and into the night, stopping only to water their horses. When they reached the city, Ishme rode with his commander to the house of the king's physician.

Lord Ninurta took one look at the general's arm and nodded. "You did the right thing by coming to me, General. I'll need to remove the rest of the shaft." Sitting in the small surgery, Ninurta handed the general a goblet of wine. Naaman swallowed it down and Ninurta said, "And another." After a few moments the physician ordered, "Bite down and do as I say!"

Naaman obeyed and tried not to cry out as the surgeon slowly removed the wooden shaft. Ishme could only watch helplessly. Naaman cried out in agony when the physician pulled it out. The nerves in his arm that the arrow blocked suddenly became excruciatingly alive and began to throb.

"Help me hold him still, Ishme," the healer ordered. He then sewed up the two wounds, front and back. Putting some salve on a linen bandage, Ishme helped him wrap it tightly around Naaman's arm. After fashioning a sling, Ninurta growled, "You are not to move this arm, General. I'll call all the gods of darkness upon you if you disobey me."

"I'll see that he doesn't my Lord," Ishme said.

"You better keep more than an eye on him, Captain," the physician growled. "Tie him down if you have to, but this is serious. Give him this powder for the pain. Put a spoonful in a cup of wine, then call me when the fever strikes." Ninurta had also been a soldier so he knew what injuries would do. "This gray powder can be used to keep the fever down and help him sleep. Just one spoon of this will do the trick."

"We understand," Naaman shouted. His arm was really hurting now. "But will I lose the strength in this arm?"

"No, General, not if you do the exercises I'll be giving you later. You should be all right. Pray the gods to make it so."

"Let's go," Naaman growled. Ishme walked with him back to his horse. Turning to the healer, Naaman said, "You have my thanks once again, my friend. I will not forget you."

"May our god Rimmon go with you, my Lord," the physician said. He was invoking the name of the principal deity of Syria. "And stay away from flying arrows."

As feared, Naaman developed a high fever, which abated in three days. Lady Adorina prayed to the small statue of Rimmon in her foyer, thanking him for sparing her husband's life. The stone god of thunder held a bolt of lightning in his hand. The people of the region had worshiped the god of lightning and rain for centuries.

Her servant Meira waited until her mistress had finished praying. "Lord Ninurta has come every day to change the bandages. He seems pleased with how well the arm is healing."

Her mistress nodded and smiled.

A short time later that morning, the physician arrived and examined his patient in the bedchamber. "Remember, General, you must keep your arm high enough so the throbbing can be controlled. It has to be higher than your heart."

"Come here Little General," the physician called to Naaman's son. "I've made a sling for you too, Ashur." When he put it on, the boy made Naaman laugh as he pretended to walk around wounded like his father, holding his arm up high.

"Just a moment," Ninurta said, examining Naaman's arm more closely. "When did this sore appear?" He pointed to the lesion that wouldn't go away.

"Perhaps six or seven months now. It's nothing. It just stays the same."

The physician looked at the spot and frowned. "I want you to come to my surgery tomorrow, General. No, I'll make it an order so you can understand. I'm not sure, but I want another healer's opinion."

"It's not serious is it?" Naaman asked.

"It could be. We'll know tomorrow. Good day General, My Lady," he said. The steward walked with him to the door.

"What is he talking about, Beloved?" Adorina asked. Her voice showed concern now for the physician's genuine alarm.

"This little wound, Dearest," Naaman said. He pointed to the small sore below his bandage.

She leaned over and looked at it up close. "It *is* strange, isn't it?" she said. "Well, Ninurta will figure it out. Come and sit with me in the garden." The children were having their nap and the couple would be alone to enjoy the shade. Their servant came out with a tray of wine, some bread and honey and Adorina asked Meira to join them.

She sensed her husband's anxiety about his arm and made a suggestion. "Meira, why don't you tell us a story to take our mind off these things? Perhaps a tale from your sacred stories—you know the ones you're always telling little Ashur."

"Of course, my Lady, that is if the General would like me to.

Naaman nodded and propped his feet up on a footstool.

"Let me tell you the story about another arrow," she began.

"Oh Meira," her mistress lamented. "Must it be about an arrow?"

"No, no, go on," Naaman said.

"This arrow, Mistress, became a signal between a king-to-be, and the crown prince of my people many years ago." Adorina saw Meira had piqued Naaman's interest and smiled as the story began about the friendship between David and Prince Jonathan.

When she finished, the shadow on the sundial had moved one quarter of the way around the disk.

The general stood up slowly. "An excellent story, Meira. Their friendship proved brave and honorable. I liked how David kept his word and honored the memory of his friend by taking care of Jonathan's son—even after the prince died in battle."

"Thank you, Master," Meira replied. She bowed her head politely as Naaman walked back into the house. Turning to her mistress she said, "Something is troubling him."

"He must return to the physician tomorrow," Adorina explained. "The healer saw something on Naaman's arm that concerned him. He'll worry about it all night."

"I'll pray for him, Mistress," Meira promised.

Lady Adorina nodded. She knew her servant would keep her word.

Little Ashur ran into the garden, disrupting their tranquility. "Look Mother," he shouted. "My arm's better." He had removed his play sling and whirled it around his head.

"Shh, Master," Meira whispered, putting her finger to her lips. "Little Atalia is still asleep. Let's go out front and I'll play kickball with you."

"Hurrah!" Ashur exclaimed. "Come on Meira."

Adorina nodded and her servant ran off laughing behind the boy.

"Well?" Naaman bellowed. He was growing impatient. The two physicians were huddled together, rapidly discussing what they had seen on the general's skin, ignoring him completely. "I'll arrest you both," he warned. That brought the healers back to their patient.

"Lord Ashai agrees with me, General. You have contracted leprosy. There's no other diagnosis or any other way to say it. The gods have condemned you to a horrible end. You must move out of your villa immediately. There can be no contact with any of your family or servants."

Lord Ashai bowed to the commander and left the room. Naaman realized the man was afraid of what his reaction might be.

"It's not possible!" Naaman shouted. "It's just a small sore."

"No, my Lord. If you look under your right arm there's another spot. This one is white in color. Your sickness is spreading. It devastates me to see them. I wish something could be done, but there's nothing." The elderly man waited for Naaman to accept what he told him. "Would you like me to tell his Majesty? You cannot return to the palace, but someone should tell the king. You can have no contact with your men or visit the barracks. You'll have to tell Ishme, my Lord."

Naaman's eyes welled up with tears. He realized the full impact of what the healer said. "You have given me a death sentence, my Lord. I'm not prepared to die this way. In battle yes, but not slowly eaten away." He slammed his fist into the wall and shouted, "Damn the gods. Why now? I have everything a man could ask for—a beautiful wife and family. But to never embrace or touch them again—no, it's too much." He brought his fist down hard on the examination table, making the healer jump. Naaman rushed out the door, leapt onto his horse and rode home.

Dismounting, he called for his steward who came running to the front door. "Call my family into the garden, Nirar. Tell them to sit down. Include the servants as well. I must speak to everyone."

28

"Yes, Master," the steward said. He ran off to carry out his orders. A few moments later he returned. "They are assembled my Lord."

Naaman walked through the front room slowly, then, out into the garden. Little Ashur wanted to run to him, but his mother held on to him. "I am sick, my friends," he began. "It is a contagious sickness and therefore none of you may come near me or touch me. I will move out of the house and camp outside the city for now. It grieves my heart to do so, but I do not want my illness to fall on any of you. Honor my decision, I beg you." He saw there were looks of shock and fear on their faces as he turned to leave.

"What is the sickness, Husband?" Adorina asked, her voice shaking.

He turned back, and in a loud, trembling voice, said "Leprosy."

Cries of horror escaped everyone's lips as Naaman hurried out to his horse.

"What are you doing?" Adorina asked, looking at Meira who had begun to tear the collar of her robe.

"It is how we mourn those who have died, my Lady." She began weeping. Little Ashur had not seen her cry before so he put his arms around her, which made her cry all the more.

Naaman made camp off the main road in a grove of oak trees. He started a fire and had unrolled his blanket in front of it. Suddenly, a twig snapped behind him and he knew someone had followed him.

"Stay away Ishme. I know it's you. You've always been a bad tracker."

"I still kill more deer than you, anyway," his friend yelled back. "How long did it take you to make that fire by the way? You haven't had to build a fire in all the years I've known you!"

"A good while," Naaman growled.

Ishme forced himself to laugh a little, and drew closer to the fire.

"I told you to keep away." Naaman said. His voice was louder this time.

"Well, you can shout all you want, but I've talked to Ninurta and as long as I don't touch you I'll be all right," Ishme said. "And besides, that's not a problem anyway since you always smell so bad. Who'd ever want to touch you?"

Naaman picked up a stone and threw it in the direction of the voice. Suddenly he heard a yelp.

"May I approach, General?" Ishme asked sincerely.

Naaman shrugged. "It's your life."

"Thank you my Lord," Ishme replied. He approached closer, rubbing his arm where the stone had struck. "I can't begin to say how sorry I am this has happened to you. You are my best friend," Ishme whispered. He couldn't look in Naaman's direction.

"Yes, well, the gods enjoy playing with us, Ishme. This must be my turn."

The captain sat down cross-legged in front of the fire. "I want to bring two of my men to stand guard close by, General. People can become angry knowing you have this illness."

"No, absolutely not. I don't want them out here."

"But my Lord, your family deserves to know you're safe," Ishme insisted. "At least let me send Ilani and Kapu here. They'll make sure no one tries to force you away. In the meantime I've brought you some supper. All you have to do is heat it up. There's wine too. If I were you, I'd drink the whole skin."

"You are a true friend," Naaman said. "But you mustn't endanger yourself or any of my men. You have to scrub down anything I've touched or handled. Please don't make me responsible for the death of my friends."

"Understood, Commander," Ishme replied. "Now do I have your permission to bring my men in the morning?"

"Very well, if you insist, but no one else. Obey me, Captain."

"As you command, my Lord." Ishme stood and walked back to his horse. When Naaman heard him ride away, he used his good arm to raise the wineskin and began drowning his sorrows with wine. He passed out on the blanket, oblivious to the pains of the world.

CHAPTER FOUR

A SERVANT'S WORD

Meira approached her mistress in the front room. "My Lady, may I tell you something my God has revealed to me?"

Lady Adorina held baby Atalia in her arms, rocking her to sleep. "Of course, Meira. What is it?"

"There is a prophet, a man of God, in my country who can heal lepers. His reputation is well known. I implore you to send the Master to him."

Adorina smiled politely, aware of the young woman's inexperience. "No one can cure leprosy, my dear. As much as I would like to believe it, it just isn't possible."

The servant sat down on the divan across from her mistress, shaking her head. She would not back down. "The man of God is the successor to Elijah, our greatest prophet, my Lady. He too healed the sick and raised the dead." She saw the disbelief on Adorina's face. "It's true my Lady. At his death, the Lord took him into heaven in a fiery chariot. The mantle of his power passed to Elisha, his adopted apprentice. We must send the general to this man, and have faith he will be healed."

Adorina stood, then walked slowly to the nursery. Meira followed, waiting while she placed the infant in her crib. Then they made their way to the kitchen, and sat down at the table, their favorite spot. Suddenly Meira saw tears in her mistress' eyes.

"If only it were true, Meira," she whispered. "But it's not. No one can do such things."

"But mistress, our sacred writings teach us that with God all things are possible. Little Ashur is proof of that isn't he?"

"Yes of course," Adorina admitted. "We were just not patient enough. The boy might have been born anyway."

"You don't believe that, do you?" Meira asked.

Her mistress shook her head. "No, I believe your god heard your prayers and we will always praise him for that."

Meira thought carefully about what to say next. "I believe this may be why the Lord led me to stay here with you and the general. The Master will die from this disease unless he gets help. Let me at least tell him, my Lady, while there is still hope."

"Very well, Meira. Captain Ishme can take you to him, but don't be upset if he refuses to see you."

"He'll see me. He likes me, ever since my first day here. He likes the way I can make him laugh."

Her mistress smiled. "It's true." After a moment she continued, "We often wondered why you chose to stay when Deborah returned home. Do you really believe it is for this reason?"

Meira looked directly into her eyes. "Yes, Mistress. I believe it with all my heart."

That afternoon when Captain Ishme came to get the general's supper and to give Adorina a report on the commander, she and Meira met him in the kitchen. Adorina told him to take Meira to her husband.

"He'll not allow it, my Lady," Ishme protested.

"Do it for me, Captain. I believe she may have the answer."

"The answer?" Ishme said. "There is no answer. Naaman has an incurable disease and that is that."

"Not so, Captain," Meira interrupted. "The God of my people has a man who can heal leprosy. If our Master goes to him he *will* be cured. I have faith to believe it, and so must you and my Lady."

Ishme became angry. "Enough. I'll take you in the morning, but the General will not see you or believe you."

"Thank you my Lord," Meira said. She left the room quietly. Her first step accomplished.

The next morning, Ishme came for her, but Meira refused to sit on the horse behind him. Instead, she walked alongside as they followed the road out of the city. It took them almost an hour to reach the guard post. Ilani and Kapu were surprised to see their captain had brought a woman.

"How is he today?" Ishme asked.

"Angry and in a foul mood," Kapu replied. "Who can blame him?"

"You stay here with the men, Meira. I'll go on ahead," Ishme said. The morning air brought a chill with it so she walked over to their fire.

Ishme went on foot into the stand of trees and approached Naaman's fire. The still air allowed Meira to hear the two men talking a short distance away.

"You're late!" the general growled.

"Yes, well I had to bring someone with me."

"What? Get him away from here!" Naaman bellowed. "I told you *no visitors*, you thick-headed son of a jackal."

"It's not a visitor, you stubborn son of a mule" Ishme shot back. It was the first time he had insulted his superior officer.

Naaman only laughed. "Then who is it?"

"Someone your Lady has sent, General. She pleads with you to listen to her."

"*Her*? Who is this woman?" He paused. "No wait, don't tell me. It's Meira isn't it? No one else would be brave enough to disobey my orders." He turned his back to his aide. "Gods! Can't I even suffer in silence?"

"Lady Adorina thinks you should hear her out," Ishme insisted. "At least listen to her—she's helped you before."

Meira didn't hear anything else so she hoped the general had agreed. When she heard Ishme's footsteps and saw his face she knew she had won. He beckoned for her to follow him.

As Meira approached the general's fire, she stopped about ten feet away as did Ishme. "I could hear you and Ishme bellowing, Lord General," she said.

"Women," he growled. "Can't you leave me alone? I allow you to come only because my wife requested it. Now you may go."

"I refuse to go until you hear the good news," Meira retorted.

"What good news? Could it be that you've decided to go back to your own country. Now that would be good news." He meant it as a joke but realized immediately he had hurt her feelings. "I didn't mean it, Meira, you know how I enjoy arguing with you."

She smiled. "This news is even better, you old bear." Naaman laughed again and she continued. "There is a holy man in Samaria, a prophet, who can cure your leprosy." She saw his shocked expression and it encouraged her to continue,.

"No one can cure leprosy. All the physicians have told me that. No one," Naaman told her.

"God can," Meira said.

"God can. What do you mean?" Naaman asked.

Ishme sat down on the grass, listening intently.

"He has given His power to a prophet. The man's name is Elisha and he can cure you my Lord, I know it."

"Forgive me Meira, but I can't believe such a claim."

"Very well, General," Meira countered. "I thought you might want to embrace your wife and children again." She turned to go. Glancing back, she saw her last words had a strong effect on her master.

Ishme approached. "What can you lose in trying to find this man, my Lord?"

"Go away and let me think," Naaman ordered. "Take her back home."

"As you command," a disappointed Ishme replied. He then turned and led Meira back toward his men. Neither felt like talking on the journey back to town. Once, when he stopped to let his horse drink at a small brook he said, "Do you know where this prophet can be found?"

"He's in the capital city, Captain," Meira replied. "King Joram will know more than anyone in Samaria how to find him. The prophet has free access to his majesty's court."

"I understand. I'll tell the General if he asks me."

When they reached home, Meira told Lady Adorina her husband seemed grateful for the news but needed time to decide what to do. "He'll come around, my Lady. You'll see."

As Meira walked toward the kitchen she heard Ishme mumble, "I'm not as certain as she, my Lady. The General's skeptical about it all."

"Now that sounds like my husband," Adorina replied. "We will give him time."

Ishme nodded. "Yes, but time is short and of great value to him." Ishme said goodnight and left the villa.

Meira approached her mistress. "He's right, my Lady. Time is his enemy now."

Adorina nodded, then went to the nursery where her children were still napping.

The following day, Ishme approached Naaman out of breath. "The king asks for you, General. The physician has told him of your condition and he orders you to meet him midday at the royal farm."

The news disturbed Naaman. "I did not want to risk infecting his majesty. Why would he command my presence?"

"I've spoken to him, General. He simply wants to see his friend. He's as devastated by the news as we all are. I think you should go to him."

"It *is* a royal command. Who am I to disobey it? He is wise in choosing the farm. At least there'll be no courtiers present."

"We still have some time before we must leave," Ishme said. "Have you given your maidservant's proposal any thought?"

Naaman frowned a little which his aide took it as a bad sign. But Naaman surprised him when he said "I will go to Samaria as soon as possible."

"Praise our Lord Rimmon, General. Your Lady also agrees. If their god has placed Meira here to help you, then it would be a sacrilege to refuse his help."

"Let me bathe and dress. I should look my best for his majesty. Ride back and bring a clean tunic and my good sandals."

"Is that all, General?"

"No, bring my helmet and breastplate as well."

"Very good. You'll need to wash out your own clothes from now on, my Lord. I'll bring some more when I return." He saluted without thinking, then rode back to town. When Ishme returned, he found Naaman sitting on a large boulder near the stream, drying himself in the sun. He placed the officer's clothes over a bush nearby, and waited for the general to get dressed. Naaman wore only his loincloth, and Ishme could see the faint white spots on the man's body. Knowing what they signified, he looked away, pained by the sight.

After pulling on his trousers, he slipped into his tunic. After affixing his breastplate, he completed his uniform by putting on his helmet. Climbing into his chariot he said, "Let's ride, Captain." They left Ilani and Kapu to watch the camp, and rode toward the hills south of the city.

"It's good to be riding with you again," Ishme said.

"For me too, but it won't be for long if this prophet can't help me," Naaman reminded him. They reached the entrance to the king's farm just as the sun reached directly overhead.

"There's his horse," Naaman said. A white stallion was tethered in front of the farmhouse. It had a black star-like mark on its forehead. As they dismounted and tied up their horses, the king came out.

"Our long-lost general has been found. Good work, Ishme," Hadadezer said.

Both soldiers bowed their heads to the king, extending their arms in a salute.

"Welcome my old and dear friend. I would embrace you, but..." and he left the rest of the words unsaid.

"My Lord and King," Naaman said, his voice betraying the emotion he felt. "I am so sorry."

"It is I who regret what has befallen you and your family, old friend. You didn't deserve such a punishment from the gods! I wish we could go inside and drink some wine together."

Ishme shook his head. "No Majesty. It would be dangerous for you both."

"Yes of course," Hadadezer replied. "Go inside and tell the servants to bring us some chairs." Ishme nodded and went into the house. When he returned, they placed them in the shade of a tall pine growing near the house. The general's aide made sure they were far enough away from the king.

Naaman removed his helmet and set it on the grass beside his chair. Before he could sit down the king said, "Will you show me, brother?"

"Majesty," Naaman replied, bowing his head. Removing his breastplate he pulled his tunic over his head. Hadadezer gasped when he saw the spots on Naaman's back, shoulders and arm. Putting the garment back on Naaman said, "There is no pain, Majesty. The gods have at least spared me that."

Tears welled up in the king's eyes. What he had seen made him angry that he was powerless to help his friend.

"Save your tears, 'Dezer," Naaman said. "There is still hope for me." He saw the startled look on his friend's face, and continued. "I want to go to Samaria, Majesty. There is a prophet of their god who can cure me. I ask only that you don't choose my replacement until I return. If I am healed, then perhaps you will let things go on as before. If not, then it is in your hands."

Looking at Ishme the king asked, "Do *you* believe there is such a prophet, Captain?"

Clearing his throat Ishme said, "I believe we must find him, Majesty. If he is as powerful as Naaman's servant says he is, then I will believe."

"A diplomatic answer if ever I heard one," Hadadezer grumbled. Turning to Naaman he said, "Then go with my permission. I will give you a letter for King Joram asking him to help find this prophet. No one will take your place while you are gone, and I swear to protect your family as my own." The king saw the tension leave his friend's body and smiled. "Ishme, come to the palace tomorrow for my letter, and may Rimmon go with you both." Unable to touch each other, Naaman and the king raised their hands in farewell.

Mid-morning the next day, Ishme returned to Naaman's hideaway with the king's letter.

Naaman gave him some new instructions. "I cannot go to the man of God without an offering. Take ten talents of silver, and at least six thousand pieces of gold from my account in the king's treasury. Put the money and ten sets of clothing in one of my iron chests and have it ready in the morning. I will come to the villa to collect it and say farewell to my family. See that one of the men brings my chariot."

"Very well, General."

"Tell our men here that I would like them to come with us, but you must ask them so they can notify their families. They may not be willing to make such a journey."

"They are yours to command, my Lord. I don't need to ask them," Ishme protested.

"I would prefer you to *ask* them this time, my friend," Naaman said. "I cannot make my men travel with me on such a mission. Coming with me will be dangerous for them, so please see to it."

"Understood."

Naaman nodded and watched Ishme walk back to the other camp. His heart beat a little faster as he realized tomorrow could be the beginning of a journey that might bring him a cure.

In the morning, as he bathed, he decided he should look his best for his family. He put on his breastplate and helmet and rode his chariot to his men's camp.

The four soldiers snapped to attention and he told them to mount up. He led the way back to his house for the first time in weeks.

Naaman smiled because little Ashur saw him first.

The boy shouted, "There's Papa! I see him!" He was standing behind the gate of the fence around the general's property.

Ishme waited in front of the house, beside the cart on which sat the iron and wooden chest. Ilani immediately dismounted and hitched the cart to his horse.

Naaman remained in his chariot so as not to be tempted to touch anyone. He spoke in a loud clear voice, "I bid you farewell this morning in the hope that Meira's prophet will be able to cure me. Pray for us while we are gone. Have no fear; the king himself told me yesterday that his guards will protect and watch over you. My love for you is stronger than it has ever been. I simply say good bye until I return."

Adorina held up little Atalia so he could see her and he smiled and waved to the baby. His wife handed their daughter to Meira so she could come closer. She wiped the tears from her eyes as she threw Naaman kisses. His son saluted him and he returned it with a flourish. Waving a last time to his family and servants, he turned his chariot around and headed down the road.

As the small group left, Ishme rode alongside the general. "I remembered to bring a royal flag of truce, General. We'll need it if we encounter any of Joram's army on the way. With a letter for their king, it makes us an official diplomatic mission."

"Good thinking, Captain," Naaman replied. "It could save our lives. Perhaps Meira's god is already beginning to watch over us."

CHAPTER FIVE

JEHORAM

"The journey to Israel's capital will take three days, my Lord," Ishme told Naaman. "The summer climate is perfect for sleeping outdoors, and it's a good thing we're all excellent archers. There'll be plenty of game for supper."

The first evening, as the five men ate together, Naaman ate alone, keeping his distance from them.

Thinking the general couldn't hear, Kala said softly, "If he doesn't find a cure, those spots will begin to get bigger. They'll turn even whiter, with a sort of shiny, scaly appearance. Pretty soon the spots will spread over his whole body and his hair will fall out—first from his head, then the eyebrows. Fingernails and toenails will become loose. They too will eventually fall off. The joints of his fingers and toes will also rot and fall off piece by piece."

"Enough," Ishme growled. "None of that's going to happen to the general. We have to believe *for* him that the god of these Israelites will cure him. Finish your supper, that is if you still have an appetite. Get some sleep. We have to be on alert tomorrow as we cross the border. Kala, because of your vivid imagination, you will have the first watch."

Naaman *had* heard every word. He gritted his teeth as Kala told them what might happen to his body. When Ishme came to say goodnight, he thought the general to be asleep, rolled up in his blanket. Naaman, however, wouldn't sleep at all that night.

Meanwhile, thirty miles away in the capital city of Samaria, King Joram, ruler of the northern kingdom of Israel, acknowledged his chamberlain.

"Your Majesty, a rider has brought word that a Syrian general bearing a flag of truce has been stopped at our border."

The king frowned, displeased with the news. "What kind of trick is that Syrian king playing now, Lord Zechariah?"

"Is he to be allowed to pass unharmed, my king?" the chamberlain asked.

The king waved his hand, "Yes, yes, of course. We don't want to provoke a war over a diplomatic envoy. This general must be bringing me an important invitation to meet with Hadadezer somewhere."

"Thank you, Majesty, I'll tell the Captain of the Guard." The chamberlain bowed before leaving the king's presence.

When the elderly chamberlain came out into the hallway Captain Eleazer asked, "What did he say?"

"They may pass without incident, Captain," Zechariah replied."

"Bah! Joram's so weak, no wonder the Syrians attack all the time. We need to stand up to them. Kill a few more of them if we want to be respected."

"In that case, young man, I'm glad you are not king. We'd be annihilated before we knew what struck us."

The Captain of the Guard mumbled something the chamberlain couldn't hear and stormed out of the palace. Zechariah had survived the turbulent reign of Ahab, Joram's father, but he was alarmed that many of the vices of the father were reemerging in the son.

The Israelite border guards stopped Naaman and his men when they crossed the Jordan River. The Syrians had planned on following the road down through the Jezreel Valley but waited for the Israelite king's permission to continue. Naaman sat by himself under a juniper tree while Ishme and the enemy officer talked.

The captain of the border patrol spoke in Aramaic, the common language between them. "Why is your commander dressed like that? It's hot today, and yet look how he covers himself."

"My general has a skin condition," Ishme replied. "He is seeking permission to be treated at the Salt Sea." Everyone knew that those who bathed in the sea received relief from their skin ailments.

The Israelite scowled. "Keep him away from us, then."

"As you will," Ishme replied.

When Ishme came back, Naaman said, "The Syrians have made us camp here since early this morning. Now it's nearly dark. If we have to wait for word from the capital, we'll be here another whole day."

"What can we do, General?" his aide asked.

"We must wait of course," Naaman said. Then, he became quiet for a moment. "That was quick thinking on your part, about the Salt Sea. I wouldn't have thought of it."

"What will happen my Lord, when the king reads the letter and learns the true nature of your sickness? Will we be shunned by him and the people?"

"I'm sure of it, so we must be prepared. I'll keep my arms covered as best I can. But people will probably throw things at us. It's to be expected."

"Your men will be angry to see you treated so, General."

"Prepare them, Ishme," Naaman said.

In the morning, an archer from each army competed to see who could bring down game for the day's meals. Samsi, one of Naaman's men, brought cheers from his comrades when he came back with two large deer. After dressing them, they roasted them and shared half with their Syrian counterparts.

"The enemy are pleased with our gesture, my Lord," Ishme said.

A rider arrived mid-morning with word from the king. He handed the message to the Captain in charge who read it and walked toward the Israelites.

"What is it?" Ishme asked.

"It's the answer your general awaits."

Naaman stood and approached the captain, stopping a good distance away. "What does it say?"

"The king gives you right of passage, my Lord, under a flag of truce," the young officer told him. "You may leave when you're ready."

"Thank you, Captain, we'll start at once." He turned back and began to roll up his blanket. His men did the same. Kapu attached his horse to the cart, and in a matter of minutes the Syrian warriors left the border outpost. Other travelers on the road recognized the enemy and moved quickly out of the way of Naaman's chariot.

Upon reaching the market at Tirzah, no one would sell to them. They left town as quickly as they could. Instead of using the wells on the way, they filled their waterskins from the clear streams that flowed down from the hills. At nightfall, they set up camp once more.

"Put two men on sentry tonight," Ishme ordered his men. "These villagers might not honor our flag of truce and could attack us as we sleep."

"I agree," Naaman said. "They see only enemy soldiers, and rightfully so. King Joram should have assigned soldiers to escort us." As they were about to settle down for the night they heard horses approaching.

"Who's there?" Ishme called out.

"Can't see, sir, it's too dark," Kapu called back.

"Don't fear," a voice shouted to them. "I am Captain Eleazer with my aide. We have been sent by his majesty to guide you to the palace."

Naaman looked at his men and smiled. "The gods must be listening."

Ishme grinned and Naaman laughed when he saw the look on his friend's face in the firelight. *"You* deal with him, Ishme. I'll go back to my blanket. I'll be able to hear you from there."

"Welcome Captain," Ishme said addressing the Israelite. "We were just turning in. Have you eaten supper?"

"Yes," the Israelite said. He moved closer to the blazing fire. "May I speak to the general?"

"He has already retired Captain," Ishme said. "Perhaps you can wait until morning."

"Very well. One of us will stay awake with your sentry. We can speak with him tomorrow as you say," Eleazer replied.

"Good," Ishme said. "This is where I'll sleep. Awaken me if there's any trouble."

"Understood, but there will be no trouble. That's why we're here," the Israelite said.

"May it be so," Ishme mumbled. He said goodnight and headed for his blanket.

"Ow," Naaman groaned as he awakened. Trying to rub his head, he found his hands and feet tied. Looking around, he saw that those of his men and the two Israelites were tied up as well. During the night, brigands must have entered the camp and knocked everyone unconscious. He saw that the iron chest had been brought near the fire.

"So," a man yelled at them. "Syrian dogs caught on our land. I say we kill 'em."

"And what about us, the king's soldiers?" Captain Eleazer shouted back. "These men are on a mission to the king and are under his protection."

"Bah! What do we care?" another spat. "All soldiers treat farmers like dogs. Why should we worry about them?"

Eleazer said, "Because what you're doing could start a war again, and that can only bring more misery—for farmer and soldier alike. What about your families?"

Ignoring the soldier's question, a second man spoke up. "What's in that box?"

Naaman quickly counted ten men in the band and for the first time felt helpless. "It's a gift for your king," he answered.

"I say we take it and break it open," the first man shouted. Five or six of the other brigands were about to rush toward the box when suddenly they were attacked by more Israelite troops. Within a few moments all the brigands lay dead.

"What took you so long, Joel?" Captain Eleazer growled. Their rescuers began cutting the ropes to free them.

"By the gods, these are *your* men, Captain?" Ishme said. "Where did they come from?"

Eleazer grinned., "Up ahead on the road. I told them if we didn't show up at sunrise they were to backtrack and see why. A smart move if I do say so."

"By Rimmon's beard," Ishme marveled. "We are in your debt, Captain, but we regret Israelites had to die."

"They were thieves and bandits," Eleazer said. "They've made traveling on this road dangerous for everyone." He paused for a moment then decided to make an observation. Nodding his head toward Naaman he said, "Your general doesn't say much, does he?"

Naaman knew he couldn't keep his secret for long. He decided the time had come to clear things up. He felt they were in the company of men who possessed a sense of duty and he walked toward the Israelites.

"I must apologize for my silence, Captain," Naaman began. "You have saved the life of King Hadadezer's General. I've come to your country to seek a cure for my illness. It is contagious, so I let Ishme speak for me. What I told the men about the chest of iron is partly true. In it is a gift for the man of god to help me find a remedy. I keep myself apart from my men to protect them. Now you know."

The enemy captain didn't know how to respond. So he simply nodded and ordered his men back to the road. "I'll join you shortly," he told them. When they were gone he turned to Naaman. "It is my duty to take you to the king and I'll see that you arrive safely. You'll have no interference from us. Leading you to Samaria is now my mission too."

Naaman said, "Thank you again, Captain. I am grateful and I will tell your king how your men saved us this day." That pleased the Israelite, and Ishme ordered his men to pack up and join up with their escort.

"We are only a half-day's journey to Samaria," Eleazer said.

By early afternoon they reached the outskirts of the ancient city, built at the foot of Mount Gerezhim. "The palace is not far," Eleazer said. "We should probably camp here until morning. The king doesn't give audiences in the afternoon."

Ishme looked at Naaman who nodded his head in agreement.

"Good," Eleazer said. "I'll send some men into town for fresh bread and wine."

Naaman walked back to the place he had chosen a little distance from the fire. Ishme came by later. "They *will* make a good escort, General. Tomorrow, if the gods will it, we will see if their king knows where the prophet can be found."

"Meira's god is still watching over us," Naaman said. "A few hours ago I thought we were all dead men." Ishme sat down on the grass some distance from his friend. "I want to talk to you about tomorrow," Naaman continued. "As a leper I won't be allowed in the city as you know. You will go for me and take the letter. Once the king has read it, he will understand why I have remained in camp."

"Yes, General, I understand," Ishme responded.

"Do all you can to learn the whereabouts of this man Elisha. My hopes go with you."

In the Samaritan royal palace, King Joram shouted at his chamberlain. "Where is he? You said the Syrian general would be here"

The older man was becoming exasperated. "Please, Majesty, he has sent his captain here in his place. The general is too indisposed to come today."

"Bring the Syrian in," Joram yelled. The guard at the door opened it and a tall warrior entered the audience chamber and knelt on one knee before the king. Saluting with his arm and fist straight out, he bowed his head.

"It is good to see a Syrian kneeling before me," Joram mumbled. He could see the young warrior appeared apprehensive, but also relieved the king had admitted him.

The king raised his hand. "Stand young man, you have our permission to speak."

Ishme stood and said clearly, "I bring greetings from His Majesty King Hadadezer, Majesty. He sends you this letter." He extended his hand containing the message and the chamberlain took it and handed it to the king.

Joram untied the ribbon and broke the wax seal. The king couldn't believe his eyes. "Listen to this Lord Chamberlain:

With this letter I am sending my servant Naaman to you so that you may cure him Of his leprosy.

"Oh," Joram cried out, tearing his gold-embroidered collar and falling to the ground. Ishme became alarmed and moved back thinking the king might be suffering from a sudden illness.

"Does he think I am God?" the king ranted. "Can I kill someone and bring him back to life? Why does this fellow send someone to me to be cured of his leprosy? You see it don't you, Zechariah? He's trying to pick a quarrel with me."

The elderly chamberlain motioned for the Syrian to leave the hall. Guards quickly opened the door so he could go out.

Lord Zechariah whispered something to the guard outside in the hall and sent him after Ishme.

The guardsman caught up with him and said, "Lord Zechariah asks you to wait here. He must speak to you."

Ishme nodded and sat down on a nearby bench beside Captain Eleazer, his escort. A short time later, the chamberlain came to them and led them to a small room Ishme assumed must be the man's office.

"Tell me, Captain, what the king is really asking. His Majesty has misunderstood the letter and I've managed to calm him for the moment."

"Our general is trying to find the prophet of your god, my Lord. He has been told the holy man will heal him."

"Ah, so that's it," Lord Zechariah sighed. "You want Elisha. Be assured the people in court today will get word to the man of God."

"Very good, my Lord," Ishme replied. "Assure his majesty that we meant no disrespect, nor wish him any harm."

"Don't worry, Captain," the chamberlain said. "The prophet will make things clear to him."

Thanking the elderly man, Ishme and Eleazer left the palace, heading back to camp.

"Your General has not been quite honest with us, Captain," the Israelite officer said. "He said he had a skin condition, but what he really has is leprosy! I can see now why he keeps to himself. At least he didn't endanger any of my men, for that I am grateful."

"We are sorry to have deceived you, Captain. We feared that if people learned of his dreaded disease, he wouldn't be allowed to pass through your country."

"I will respect his wishes, and so will my men." Eleazer replied.

"This man Elisha," Ishme said as the two men reached the outskirts of town, "do you believe he can heal my general?"

"He is a man of God, and we Israelites believe our God can do anything. It all depends on our faith. We'll have to wait and see." He paused to think how to say his next words. "First of all, you are Gentiles. Elisha may choose not to receive you at all. Who knows? Prophets can be quite unpredictable."

When Ishme returned, he told Naaman what had happened in court. The general became despondent and asked to be left alone.

"Don't worry, General," Ishme told him. "Chamberlain Zechariah told me that Elisha would hear about my visit. The courtiers will not keep it quiet that a Syrian general is seeking him out. If he feels it is the god's will, then you will receive word."

"I'm grateful to you for today, Captain," Naaman said. Removing his sandals he sat down on a large boulder.

"I became worried there for a moment when the king became so emotional," Ishme said. " I only hope for your sake this prophet is all we expect him to be."

"Pray it is so. Meira said that with her god, all things are possible."

Ishme walked over to where he had placed his blanket. He began to chuckle and Naaman asked him what he had found so amusing.

"I think the king became distressed, General, because he thought you were expecting the *king* to heal you. No wonder he became alarmed." He laughed some more, then added, "It also showed me how much he fears our great king. He feared that if *he* didn't heal you there would be another war."

"I see," Naaman said quietly. "The poor man."

"The chamberlain said we must wait. It is for Elisha to make contact with us, my Lord."

Naaman nodded. He prayed it would be soon.

CHAPTER SIX

TAKING THE PLUNGE

Back in the capital of Samaria, Lord Zechariah was nervous as he brought Captain Eleazer with him to the king's residence. "Majesty. You have received a message from the prophet."

"So," Joram sighed, "We hear from him at last. Hand it to me."

The chamberlain gave him the small scroll, but the king suddenly put his hand up. "No! No, you read it for me," he said, giving it back. "If it's a curse, let it fall on you and not me"

Zechariah frowned but unrolled the small piece of parchment. "Elisha says,

'Why have you torn your robes? Send the man to me and he will know that there is a prophet in Israel.'

"What?" Joram mused, "is that it?"

"Yes, Majesty," the chamberlain said. "The servant who brought the message said he would lead this general to the prophet. You will be finished with this matter."

Captain Eleazer became uneasy when the king stared at him.

"I want all Syrian soldiers out of my kingdom at once," the king ordered.

"Yes, Lord King," the elderly man agreed. "I will send Elisha's servant with Captain Eleazer at once." The king waved his hand in dismissal and both the courtier and the Israelite officer left the king's presence.

In the long polished granite corridor, the two men approached a man sitting near the doors of the palace.

Lord Zechariah turned to the officer and said, "This man is the prophet's servant. He will take you to him."

"As the king commands," Eleazer answered with a salute. He motioned for the servant to follow him and went down the steps to his horse.

"I have a mule," the servant said. "I'll follow you, Captain." Eleazer set off at a moderate pace so the mule could keep up. A half-hour later they reached Naaman's camp.

"This is Elisha's servant, my Lord," Eleazer said. "He is our guide to the man of God."

"*Our* guide?" Naaman asked, surprised.

"Yes, we will come with you for your protection."

Naaman thought a moment. "I welcome your presence, Captain. I appreciate your dedication to duty. Prepare the cart, Captain Ishme. We leave at once."

Eleazer watched as Ishme hitched his horse to the cart. "How far away is it?" the Syrian officer asked.

"Not far," was all Elisha's servant would say. They now made up a company of sixteen, and Naaman felt embarrassed to have so many people going with him to the holy man.

After a short journey, the servant guided his mule down a narrow path that led to a very humble dwelling. It was a stone house like the others on the road and had a flat roof. A small vineyard grew beside it.

Naaman was not sure this could be the right house. "The prophet lives here?"

"Yes my Lord, for about three years now," the servant said. "Wait here." The man jumped off his mule, and went down the path and into the house.

"My companions will not go inside if invited," Naaman told Eleazer.

The captain nodded. The Israelite knew that this would be the general's moment. He would not want them in there with the holy man. Naaman dismounted and waited patiently. Suddenly, a well-dressed man came out and everyone wondered if he might be Elisha.

"I am Gehazi, my Lords, Elisha's aide. He knows why you have come and has sent me with instructions."

"Instructions?" Naaman said. "The holy man will not see me?"

"No, my Lord," Gehazi said. "He instructs you to go wash yourself in the Jordan River seven times. Your flesh will be restored and cleansed."

Eleazer saw Naaman's face change. All the muscles in his face became tense and he stomped toward his chariot. "By the gods!" he shouted. Climbing back into it he yanked the reins and drove off—not waiting for Ishme or his men.

"Where is he going?" Eleazer asked.

Ishme unhitched the cart and took Ilani and Kapu with him in pursuit of their leader. The startled Israelite escort followed right behind.

"I've found him," Kapu shouted. He pointed toward a small stream outside the city where the general had abandoned his chariot.

Naaman ignored them. He shouted curses at the sky and struck one of his horses' hindquarters when the animal came too close.

Finally, sitting down on a log he said, "I thought Elisha would come out to me and stand and call on the name of the Lord his god, perhaps even wave his hand over my sores and cure me."

His men could hear the anger and disappointment in his voice.

Eleazer looked at Ishme, who only shook his head. The Israelite officer guessed the captain had seen his general this way before, so he and his men dismounted and sat on large rocks beside the stream.

"Wash in the Jordan? Can you believe it?" Naaman ranted. "Aren't the rivers of Damascus—the beautiful Abana and the Pharpar—better than any of their rivers? Couldn't I wash in *them* and be cleansed?" He stopped shouting to catch his breath. After a moment he yelled, "I'm so angry I could kill a whole regiment by myself!"

Eleazer smiled. Ishme and his men were wise enough to let their general vent his anger. "We've come all this way and risked our lives, and for what?" Naaman went on. "I've never been so insulted in my life. Doesn't he know who

I am? Yet he treats me this way!" When he had exhausted himself, he sat down and his men joined him. Eleazer and Ishme simply watched and listened from where they were.

When Ishme saw the general was through, he spoke up. "General, you are like a father to us, but you are not thinking clearly. If the prophet had asked you to do something difficult, wouldn't you have done it? He has given you a simple command, 'wash and be cleansed.'"

Ilani spoke up, "Please Lord General. You must at least do what he tells you for Lady Adorina's sake and your children."

Naaman suddenly felt his face turning red. He was embarrassed for acting like a spoiled child.

At that moment, two of his men arrived pulling the cart behind them. Ishme had forgotten the valuable chest and was relieved when he saw it.

"How far is the Jordan River from here, Captain?" Naaman asked Eleazer.

The Israelite grinned. "That's more like it, General. We've learned after many defeats, that the Lord our God requires faith and obedience." He saw a look of understanding on Naaman's face. "I know a faster way down to the Jordan. It'll take only a few hours to get there. We can go in the morning."

Naaman smiled. "You would think a general, of all people, should know about obedience, Captain. Let's return to camp, and leave in the morning."

The warriors of both armies relaxed, glad the general had come to his senses.

Eleazer overhead one of Naaman's men say, "For a moment there, I really believed he would go back to Damascus."

Captain Ishme grinned. "So did I, soldier."

Naaman awoke before anyone else, hopeful the new day would bring his cure. He didn't think the prophet's request had been unreasonable. It might seem simple and foolish, but decided to do what the prophet told him.

The morning chill remained, even though the summer sun had been up a short time. A rooster crowed in the distance, but by then all the men were up. Someone made a fire and men from both camps began their daily routine of bathing and cooking.

Ishme greeted his leader. "Today is a fine day to be healed, General." He had walked over to where Naaman had slept, some distance from his men.

"It is indeed," Naaman replied. "I pray Meira's god will honor the prophet's words." As he washed himself he still could not feel any pain, even though the sores had gotten worse. He could only imagine how his back and shoulders must look.

After a short time they were ready, and Naaman had become conflicted about the iron box. They couldn't leave it here, so he finally decided to bring it along with them.

"Here's the shepherd's path, General," Eleazer said. He led the way down the hill, and villagers on the path moved aside to let them pass. Since the descent proved difficult for the chariot and their animals, they stopped from time to time to let the horses rest and graze in the long green grass.

"Once we're over the next hill we should be able to see the river valley," Eleazer told them.

Naaman sat under a juniper tree, reluctant to share what he had been thinking, but decided to do so anyway. "Your country is beautiful, Captain. Our land as you know, is more arid and rocky. Your god has blessed this land."

"And yet we take it for granted," the Israelite said. "We complain endlessly about how much better off the sea people are, or you people in the north. We are never happy where we are."

"It's a human weakness, I believe," Naaman said. "We do not know how good our lives truly are until we are about to lose them."

"You're right, my Lord," Eleazer said. "I shall appreciate this day for what it will bring."

Naaman nodded and got back on his horse as the company continued down the winding path. The descent was not easy in the chariot and Naaman had to hold on to the railing.

"There it is," one of Eleazer's men shouted a short time later. Naaman looked at the misty-blue haze over the Jordan, clearly visible now. They'd reach the water before long.

"We're almost there," Ishme said. "I pray all the gods bless you, my friend."

Naaman shook his head. "I've given up on all the other gods." He paused a moment before saying, "I'm praying the god of Elisha will bless me."

At the riverbank, the Syrians were surprised to see how much narrower the river seemed from where they had crossed several days ago. "It's not very deep nor far across," Ilani observed. "It's not as great or as powerful as the Abana back home." Tying their horses to small shrubs growing along the bank, they waited for orders.

Naaman watched as Captain Eleazer encouraged his men to camp together under several large willow trees.

"We'll give the Syrians some space, men," their officer told them. "This is a special moment for the general and we'll honor his privacy." His men grumbled and were not pleased. They *wanted* to see what would happen to Naaman!

Naaman's men camped on the riverbank, waiting for him to enter the water. "Ishme," Naaman called, "you will count for me. In my excitement, I may lose count."

"As you command, my Lord."

Naaman removed his tunic and shirt, but kept on his breeches. He saw his aide flinch at the sight of the sores.

"Here I go," Naaman said. He waded waist deep into the muddy stream, shivering from the cold water. He bent his knees, putting his whole body under water. He remained submerged for as long as he could, then came back up. Looking first at his arm, he was disappointed. He could see no change. He stood up straight and shook his head, trying to get the water out of his ears.

"Again, General," Ishme shouted.

Naaman closed his eyes and went under a second time, holding his breath. Then standing once more—he looked and still no change.

"Down for three," his friend called to him. The general's men walked closer and stood behind Ishme. They watched as their general went under once again.

"Any change, my Lord?" Ishme called.

Naaman shook his head.

"This will be four, my friend."

The general nodded, then slowly immersed himself again.

When he came up the fourth time, he felt discouraged because his arm remained the same. There had been only a slight stinging on his shoulders where there were many open sores.

"Let's try for five, my Lord General," Ishme called.

"Don't give up, General," Kapu shouted, forgetting himself. Naaman smiled and shook his head, hitting one side of his head with the heel of his hand, trying to get the muddy water out of both ears. This time he sat down in the water, lowering himself as far down as he could go. He held his breath longer, thinking perhaps he needed to stay under for a more extended time.

When he came up slowly, Ishme said, "Just two more, my Lord. Is anything happening?"

Naaman looked, then shook his head. His men could see the look of despair and disappointment on his face.

"This is six," Naaman declared, determined to stay under even longer. After what seemed an eternity, he gradually stood again and waited for the water to roll off before looking at his arm.

He examined the skin closely. "No change," he reported.

The Israelite soldiers, anxious to see, moved over behind the Syrians. Captain Eleazer stood next to Ishme.

"This is the last one, General," Ishme called out.

Naaman stood looking down at the water. He prayed softly this time, just above a whisper so no one could hear him. "God of Elisha and my faithful servant Meira, hear my prayer. Heal me of this leprosy and I will worship you all my days." Those were his only words. Looking at those on shore who wanted the best for him, he went down a seventh time. As he remained submerged, he felt a tingling in his whole body, a sudden wonderful sensation. It was like the good feeling one gets when a persistent itch is scratched. This time he jumped up and shot out of the water.

He looked quickly at his arm then shouted at the top of his voice—"they're gone! Look!" he yelled, "my sores are gone!" As he rushed out of the water his men backed up, suddenly afraid of him. Naaman just stood there, feeling his shoulders and reaching around to his back.

When his men saw him healed, they rushed over.

"It's true, General," Ishme shouted, laughing. "The leprosy's gone!"

"Praise the Lord God," Eleazer shouted, as did all of the Israelites. They were so excited they clapped their hands and jumped into the water, splashing and acting like little boys.

Just to make sure, Naaman ran back into the water, removed his breeches and checked his legs and body all over. Then pulling them back on, he left the river and sat on the grass to dry himself in the sun.

"Let's send for some wine, General," Eleazer suggested. "We must celebrate this great miracle! People will not believe us when we tell them. But we've seen it with our own eyes. There is no God like our God, and He is greatly to be praised."

"He is indeed, Captain," Naaman said. "I'm beginning to believe that the gifts I've brought for your prophet are not enough. How much is a life truly worth? He's given me back mine. What *could* I possibly give him?"

"We'll get the wine and camp here tonight. In the morning we'll return to Elisha," Ishme suggested.

Naaman knew his men were as excited as he and deserved a celebration. "Yes, send for wine," he shouted. "We'll drink to our good health—all of us, including me this time."

The men laughed, happy for him as he gave coins to Eleazer, who sent his men toward the nearest settlement.

That night, after a delicious meal of roast duck and plenty of wine, the men sang and danced around the campfires. They took turns teaching each other old war chants and love songs.

Too excited to sleep, Naaman spent a long time running his hand over his arm, admiring the new baby-like skin. The wonderful itching of his shoulder told him everything had healed. He couldn't wait to get home to show his beloved. He knew he had eaten too much and enjoyed too much wine. His euphoria, however, came from the joy of the miracle.

The next morning, Naaman slept longer than usual and awoke to see his men washing themselves in the river. Usually they didn't stay that long in the water. When they came out he asked Ishme what they had been doing.

"The men believe if they wash in the water that healed you, my Lord, then any of the illness you may have accidentally given them will be cleansed, too. The current will carry it away like it did yours."

Naaman was forced to smile and nodded his head. "Being around a leper can do that to you." He laughed as he watched the men cavorting in the Jordan.

When they were ready, the small caravan left the river and began the gradual climb up the shepherd's path once more. For the first time in a long while Naaman rode with his men around him. He joked with them again and they were pleased to have him back with them in the land of the living.

"When we get back, Captain Eleazer, I must go meet this holy man and thank him," Naaman said. "Can you convince him to see me this time?"

"I can only try, General," the Israelite said. "Like our Lord God, the prophet's ways are not our ways. He can refuse kings and peasants alike. I'll do my best."

"Fair enough," Naaman said. "That's all I can ask." As they rode on, Naaman began to wonder. "How does your prophet earn a living? Does the king pay him, or the priests?"

"No one pays him, my Lord," Eleazer explained. "He'll accept food and clothing from those he has helped. He relies on the Lord God to take care of him—like the birds of the air."

"Does that mean he might refuse my gifts? Surely not," Naaman asked.

"I can't say, General. If he permits you to meet him, you can only do what your heart tells you to do. He'll know you are grateful."

They stopped to rest near a spring. As they waited patiently while a shepherd watered his flock ahead of them, it gave them time to ask questions about the invisible God of Israel. Eleazer told them about their ancestor Abraham and the history of his descendants.

"Even after all these years, Captain, your God still watches over you," Naaman said. "Is King Joram a faithful follower of your God's teachings?"

"No, General, I'm afraid he is not. Many of our kings have been opposed to the Lord's prophets, and Joram has followed in his father's bad ways. Elisha has not been pleased with him, and has told him so. The king has done nothing against the prophet because he is afraid of the man."

"What happened to me today at the river has made me a believer. I want to learn more about this faith, this man Elisha, and your God."

"Then I pray my God will continue to bless you, General. Let us pray we never have to meet on the battlefield," Eleazer said.

"Let it be so." Naaman made a fist and extended his arm in a salute.

After the shepherd finished watering his sheep, the men gave water to their horses and continued up through the hills, hoping to reach the home of the prophet before dark.

CHAPTER SEVEN

ELISHA

Elisha saw the Syrians returning. From his vantage point on the roof, he could tell that Captain Eleazer led the way. He walked down the steps and found Gehazi working in the garden.

"The Syrian is back, and Eleazer is with him. I'll meet him on the roof, Gehazi."

"Yes, my Lord." His servant bowed his head, and walked through the house and stood outside the front door." Elisha walked up the stone stairs and leaned over the railing so he could hear.

Naaman and four of his men carried a strongbox and approached the front entrance. The servant opened the door and bowed his head to the general.

"I wish to see the prophet if I may," Naaman began. "I want to thank him for healing me."

"The Lord be praised," Gehazi declared.

"My praise is even greater," Naaman said. He couldn't help but smile.

"Follow me, gentlemen," the servant said. He led them up the back steps to the flat roof. He called back down to Captain Eleazer and told him he and his men could make themselves comfortable in the garden.

When he reached the top of the stairs, Naaman and Elisha saw each other for the first time. The prophet sat in the shade of two tall palm trees that grew next to the house. Elisha was dressed in ordinary homespun, and his feet were bare. His gray and white hair, and his long beard was combed but not trimmed. Elisha looked at the foreigner and smiled.

Naaman knelt on one knee and saluted the man of God. Suddenly, and without him being consciously aware at first, tears began to stream down his cheeks. "I am healed, my Lord Elisha," he said. "Look. My skin is as new as a baby's!"

Elisha raised his hands to the sky. "May the Almighty be praised. Blessed be His Name." The prophet's voice trembled and was filled with emotion.

Naaman stood. "I know now that there is no God in all the world except in Israel." The prophet didn't respond but simply nodded his head. "Please accept a gift of thanksgiving from your servant." Naaman motioned to his men to bring the box. Using a key, he opened it—showing the gold and silver coins and new clothing.

Elisha's aide, Gehazi's eyes grew larger when he saw inside the box.

At first, Elisha didn't react. Then, standing, he walked over to the box and closed the lid. He looked the general closely in the eye. "As surely as there is a living Lord, whom I serve, I will not accept a thing." He then returned to the stone bench where he had been sitting.

"Please my Lord Prophet. I do not mean to offend," Naaman said. "I know your work is for the Lord. I implore you to use these gifts to help your people."

The elderly man shook his head, smiled again and waved his hand, as if telling him to take it away.

"Remove it, Men," Naaman ordered. His four companions moved forward, picked up the heavy chest and carried it back down to the cart. Elisha watched as the general seemed hesitant to leave. Turning toward the prophet, Naaman asked, "Will you tell me more about your God, my Lord? I would make him my God."

"Tell me," Elisha began, "how did you know to come to Israel, General? Our people have been enemies for many years. How is it you come to us for help?" He motioned for the Gentile to sit down on a bench across from him.

"It was our servant girl Meira, my Lord," the Syrian explained. "We captured her during one of our raids and brought her to Damascus. My wife and I have grown to love her as one of the family. She prayed to her God for us at every crisis. I owe your God for the gift of a son and daughter because of her prayers." He paused and saw Elisha nodding his head as he told the story. "When the physicians told me I had leprosy a month ago, they gave me no hope, but Meira wouldn't give up. She told me about you, Lord Prophet. She said a man in Israel could heal me, and she spoke the truth!"

Elisha nodded. "She is well-named, your servant, my son. ' Meira' means 'giver of light.' That is what she has done, she has led you to the light."

"Let it be so," Naaman recited. "It is strange, Holy One. She actually believes your God meant her to stay in our service for this very miracle. I set her and her companion—a girl named Deborah—free two years ago, but she said the Lord told her to stay. She believed we needed her."

"And you did," Elisha said. He smiled at the Syrian and then he stood and paced around the rooftop for a moment before stopping in front of the soldier. "As you may or may not know, General, we Israelites do not normally associate with Gentiles—our word for non-believers. But I believe today, as Meira believes, that the Lord is working in your heart and that is a good thing. Many Gentiles have come to the Light of God and for that I rejoice."

Naaman felt his face flush. The prophet's kind words pleased him.

"Now," Elisha continued, "tell me about yesterday, and your cleansing at the river."

Naaman began and became more enthusiastic describing each time he plunged into the water. When he got to the seventh time, the healing itself, including how all the soldiers jumped into the water for joy, Elisha laughed and clapped his hands. "Such a day," he exclaimed.

Naaman continued. "On the way back, my Lord, Captain Eleazer told me some of the history of your people—beginning with Abraham up to the present with king Joram."

The prophet frowned at the mention of the king's name and shook his head. "An unworthy leader of our people," he growled. "The Lord is not pleased with that one."

Naaman frowned.

"Let me tell you what pleases the Lord, young man," Elisha said. He then began to teach the Gentile the ways of the Lord. Halfway through, Gehazi brought his master and his guest some wine and fresh dates.

Captain Ishme and his men waited patiently down in Elisha's garden. When they heard Gehazi come back down, Ishme asked, "What are they talking about?"

"The prophet is giving instruction to your commander about the ways of our God."

"I see," Ishme said.

"What will the general do with the chest of coins and clothing, Captain?" Gehazi asked. "That is, now that the prophet has refused them?"

The question surprised Ishme and his eyebrows went up. "I don't presume to know," he answered. "Perhaps Naaman will take it back with him."

The servant nodded and went back inside the house.

"Gehazi," Elisha called.

The man hurried out and ran up the stairs.

"Send for Jeremiah the scribe at once," the prophet ordered.

"Yes my Lord," Gehazi answered. He hurried back down and sent the prophet's gardener to go for the scribe.

When Jeremiah arrived a short time later, he was told to go on up to the rooftop.

"Come up, Ishme," Naaman called down to his aide, and the captain followed the scribe up the steps. Jeremiah bowed his head to the prophet, as did Ishme.

"Friend Jeremiah," Elisha said. "I need a scroll of the Laws of Moses to give my new friend. If you have one, can you bring it here today? There is not enough time to make such a copy. I know how particular you are with your transcriptions." Turning to the general he explained. "Writing down the sacred words is an act of worship, General. It is something that is done very carefully and reverently."

"I have such a scroll, Master," Jeremiah said. "I'll bring it for you."

"Excellent," Elisha said. "You are a good man, Jeremiah."

The scribe nodded again and hurried away.

Naaman introduced Ishme and Elisha invited him to be seated as well.

"You'll need to give Jeremiah a coin for his work, General."

Naaman nodded and the prophet continued. "I want you to study our teachings—that's what the word Torah means. They are the teachings of Moses, servant of the Lord. You will grow in the knowledge of the Light of God. I know too, if you share the scroll with Meira, she will enjoy hearing the words again. It is unusual for us to do this. In our religion, only the priests handle such sacred texts. But for now, you will be a caretaker of these holy words, bringing light to those in your country."

"I am honored and truly grateful, holy Prophet," Naaman said. He then asked, "Captain Eleazer told me there are 'righteous Gentiles' in your faith. Who then can become a righteous Gentile, my Lord?"

Elisha answered. "To become a true son of the covenant, the requirement is very personal." He went on to explain the significance of the sign of Abraham. As they talked late into the afternoon Elisha began to admire the foreigner. He had a quick mind and truly believed the Lord had healed him. When Jeremiah returned with the scroll, the three men came down to the garden where Naaman's and Eleazer's men had been waiting.

"May I come again in the morning, my Lord Prophet, to bid farewell and ask your blessing?" Naaman asked.

"Yes," Elisha answered. "Go in peace."

"May you dwell in peace," Naaman answered, as Eleazer had taught him.

The next morning when Naaman returned, Gehazi led his men into the garden once more.

Naaman took Eleazer aside and said, "I've read the laws of Moses all night. I couldn't sleep, I was so moved by the words. They are good laws and it would take a great people to follow God's commands." Speaking in a more quiet tone, he asked Eleazer, "Tell me about this sign of the covenant."

The Israelite nodded. "If you are serious my friend, it is something you can have done when you are home. I would only say it is a serious act of faith."

"I understand," Naaman said. "There are other cultures that practice it such as the Egyptians. I'll have to think about it a great deal more." Just then, the prophet came out to join them.

He raised his hand. "Blessings on you men," he said.

"Good morning, Lord Prophet," Naaman replied. He bowed his head, as did everyone in the garden.

"Have you had time to read any of the Law?" Elisha asked.

"I have, my Lord, and I like what I've read. I pray I can live up to all your God requires. I've come now to bid you farewell. I can never forget what your God has done for me. Look at my arm, my shoulder and back. But even more, I feel that He has healed my heart."

"I believe you. Your words are sincerely spoken, Naaman of Damascus," Elisha said. His voice was deep and strong. "I will pray for you and your safe return to your loved ones. Give Meira especially my blessing and greeting."

Naaman then surprised the man of God. "I ask that you allow me to take back as much earth from your garden as a pair of donkeys can carry, my Lord. I will never again make burnt offerings or sacrifices to any other God but the Lord God of Israel." He saw the look of astonishment on his teacher's face, but he had not finished. "I also thought about this long and hard. I ask you to forgive me this one thing. When my master the king enters the temple of Rimmon to bow down, as his Right Hand I must bow also. When I do, may the Lord forgive your servant for it."

Elisha, surprised by both requests needed a moment to think.

Naaman knew it a common practice of all countries around Syria to take sacred soil from holy places. He believed if he could do this, he would continue to have the presence of the God of Elisha at his home. The prophet nodded and the Syrians brought in the two donkeys and filled sacks with dirt from the garden. They placed them on the beasts of burden.

"Shalom, go in peace my son," Elisha said. Then he raised his hands and prayed a benediction upon Naaman and his family. He concluded by praying, "Go with these men, O Lord, and keep them from harm. May they be used to bring light to the Gentiles in their distant land."

"May it be so," the Israelite and Syrian soldiers said together.

Elisha walked with Naaman to the gate of his yard and watched the company of men begin their journey back up the road,

As Naaman made his way from the prophet's house, Ishme complained. "Those two donkeys are going to slow us down, General. It's just ordinary dirt. Why is it so important to you?"

"Well, *Captain*," Naaman said, reminding the officer of his place. "I will not feel right bowing down to Rimmon or any other god ever again. When I pray to the God of Israel from now on, it will be on this soil. It will remind me what the Lord did here—can you understand?"

Ishme grinned. "No, but Captains are not supposed to understand Generals, are they? I admire you, my Lord, now more than ever. I'll take care of the two beasts for you."

"Good. Now, shall we return to our camp, or head for home?"

Captain Eleazer overheard Naaman's question. "I recommend you camp one last night here, General. We can follow the path down to the Jordan again where you were healed. You can cross the river there, without going through another border control."

"A good suggestion, Captain. We will leave first thing in the morning then. We are most grateful for your rescue and help every day we've been here. We've almost become friends."

When they reached their camp, the Israelite warriors helped the Syrians purchase bread, wine, vegetables, and some apples for their return.

Captain Eleazer took Naaman aside to speak to him while their men built a fire. "I want you to know, General, that if we were to ever meet on the battle-field, I would find it hard to kill you. If you become a son of the covenant, how could I? You already have on your body the mark where the Lord healed you. Soon all of Israel will know your story. You will be as famous as Elisha, and I will not fight you."

Naaman felt touched by the younger man's words. "I too feel as you," he said. "You rescued us that first day, and it has been your help we've received everyday we've been here. I could not fight you, Eleazer, even if my king has me executed."

Eleazer smiled his biggest smile. "Well, we'll have to do all we can to make sure our two nations never fight each other again."

"Let's make it so," Naaman agreed. Then, they both burst out laughing. "As if anyone would ever listen to us!".

Ishme walked over to the general's fire. "We're being followed, General."

"Who is it?" Naaman asked.

"I can't tell, he's still far away. One of the Israelites said he's been behind us all the way."

"Let's wait until he gets here."

"Very good. I'll ask Eleazer to find out who it is," Ishme said. A little later, Eleazer came to the general with the news.

"It's the prophet's servant Gehazi, General. He won't tell me what he wants, but insists on speaking only to you."

CHAPTER EIGHT

GEHAZI

Elisha's most trusted servant followed the Syrian soldiers, hoping to get a chance to speak with Naaman. He felt his master shouldn't have been so hard on the general. He should have accepted the gifts the general brought him. He saw where the soldiers of both armies had set up camp and stopped short on the dusty road to gather his thoughts. "By the Living God I'm going after him to get something from him," he said out loud.

When he reached the camp, he was surprised when Naaman came out to meet him. Normally, people of importance, especially military commanders expected inferiors to handle such matters.

"Is everything all right?" the general asked.

"Yes everything is fine, my Lord," Gehazi said.

Naaman invited him to enter their camp and sit down on a large log near the fire.

"Something is wrong. I can see it by your expression. Tell me what it is."

Gehazi relaxed now, convinced he could fool the enemy general. "My master has sent me with a message for you, my Lord," he lied.

"Yes? What does the holy man say?" Naaman asked.

"My master has been surprised by the unexpected arrival of two young men from the school of the prophets in Ephriam. He wondered if you could give them some assistance. Perhaps a talent of silver?"

Naaman stood and looked thoughtful for a moment. He *had* wanted to give the prophet some kind of gift. Perhaps he could please the prophet by being generous to these novices. "Not just one talent of silver, Gehazi," he replied, "I insist it be two talents and two suits of clothing."

"That is very generous my Lord General." Gehazi could not believe his good fortune.

"I'll send Ilani and Kapu back with you to help carry the silver," Naaman declared. "Please tell Lord Elisha I am more than willing to help the Lord's servant."

Gehazi bowed his head with respect. "I will tell him. He will be most grateful."

Naaman asked, "Will you stay and return in the morning?"

"No, General," the man replied. "I must return with your gifts or Elisha will think something's happened to me."

"All right," Naaman replied. He called for his men who put the bags of silver over their horses and offered to give Gehazi a ride, but he said he would rather walk.

"Go in peace," Naaman said.

"Rest in peace," Gehazi responded. Then, turning away, he led the way back.

"I'm going with those two," Eleazer suddenly announced, getting up onto his horse. "You never know who they might meet, and that's a lot of silver, General."

"You're right of course," Naaman answered. The captain saluted, and rode off to catch up with Gehazi.

Elisha sat quietly on the rooftop. His eyes closed and he began to meditate on recent events. He had been pleased with how the Lord had directed him to deal with the Syrian officer, and the man seemed genuinely sincere in his desire to follow the Lord God of Israel. Suddenly, he called to Caleb his gardener.

"Where has Gehazi gone, my son?" Elisha asked.

"I don't know, Master. I saw him walking up the road a long while ago. He didn't say anything."

"Most unusual. He always tells me where he is going." With a frown he shook his head. Looking at Caleb he asked, "How are my vines doing this year, my friend?"

"I've kept them watered, Master," Caleb said. "They have been blossoming and there should be a good crop if the Lord is willing."

"Let it be so," Elisha said. He was relieved to hear it. His small vineyard did not do very well last year. His harvest hadn't been large enough to be worthy of selling to wine merchants, but he did enjoy drinking his homemade wine the rest of the year.

"Thank you, Caleb. That will be all. Tell your wife I send my greeting, and to little Isaac too."

His gardener bowed his head and went back downstairs.

Elisha mumbled to himself. "I remember the look on Gehazi's face when I refused Naaman's gifts. He wasn't pleased with me." He talked to himself more often now that his wife Galia had gone to be with the Lord. He found himself speaking to her as if she were there. She had fallen off a cart in front of their house. There was nothing anyone could do—even his mentor Elijah could not comfort him when she died. That had happened ten years ago and he still felt the pain of it.

He sat down again and laid his head on a cushion he had placed at the edge of the small railing. He looked up at the clear blue sky and within minutes dozed off. He dreamed that he saw Gehazi talking to Naaman and accepting gifts from him. The Syrians were carrying the gifts back toward the house and Elisha became agitated. When the screech from a low-flying hawk awakened him, he saw the raptor swoop down on an unsuspecting hare running in the field next to his vineyard.

"The Lord has seen you, Gehazi," the prophet exclaimed. It saddened him to see that his faithful servant had failed this most important test of faith.

As Gehazi reached the top of the hill nearest the prophet's house, he stopped and spoke to Ilani and Kapu. "I'll carry the general's gifts from here. It's only a short distance and I can carry the silver over each shoulder. I don't think my master would be pleased to have his neighbors see him accepting gifts from the enemy—no insult intended, of course."

Captain Eleazer, surprised by the remark, didn't respond. The two soldiers passed the sacks of silver to Elisha's servant who placed them over his shoulder. He carried the two changes of clothing over his arm and continued with some difficulty down the small road.

"You men wait here for me," the captain instructed. "Something's not right about this. I smell a rat in the granary." The two Syrian soldiers nodded and dismounted, leading their horses to a shaded area where passersby would not see them.

"I'll leave my horse with you," Eleazer added, "and go on foot."

"What's wrong, Captain?" Ilani asked.

"I don't know yet, but that servant is up to no good."

They nodded, and Eleazer waited until Gehazi couldn't see him before continuing slowly down the path to Elisha's house.

Gehazi went through the side entrance where he thought no one would see him. He went directly to his room and hid Naaman's items in a wooden wardrobe. Washing the dust from his hands and feet, he then went up on the roof to see his master.

As Gehazi approached, the prophet asked, "Where have you been?"

"Nowhere, Master," the man said. He kept his head down, not able to look at the prophet. "Your servant hasn't gone anywhere."

"I see." The man of God sighed with disappointment. "I received a vision in which I traveled with you on the road back to Naaman's camp and he came out to greet you."

The servant realized he had been found out and fell to the ground in front of his Master, filled with fear.

"Is this the time to take money?" Elisha asked.

Gehazi trembled, aware that the prophet of the Most High had the power of life and death.

Elisha turned away from the man and walked to the edge of his roof. In a loud voice he pronounced sentence on his unfaithful servant: "Naaman's leprosy will now cling to you and your descendants forever."

"No, Master, no," the man cried. Standing, he felt a sudden pain in his left arm—the same arm where leprosy started on Naaman. As he looked, a small white spot began to grow on the skin. A stabbing pain struck his shoulders and back and he knew the prophet's curse had begun to ravage his body. His skin turned white and Gehazi ran from the roof. In his haste to get away, he almost bumped into Eleazer at the garden gate. The captain quickly backed away from him when he saw the leprous sores on Gehazi's arms and face. Eleazer waited a moment before continuing on to Elisha's house.

"The captain's coming back," Ilani said. "What's he carrying?"

"Can't tell yet," Kapu answered. As the Israelite drew closer, they could see the changes of clothing draped over the officer's shoulder.

Eleazer said, "You're not going to believe this, but I've heard it from the prophet's own mouth!"

When he told them what had happened, Kapu said, "By the gods!" Then he knew he had insulted the captain's religion and added, "Forgive me, Captain. I just can't believe it!"

"Nor can I," Eleazer replied. "Let's get back to your general and tell him what has happened." Remounting their horses, they galloped back to camp. The sun sank lower on the horizon and it would be dark in a short time.

When Eleazer dismounted back at camp, Naaman saw the new clothing. "What's wrong?" he asked.

"You need to sit down, General," the captain said. "You're not going to believe me."

"He's right," Ilani added.

Kapu nodded in agreement.

"It has all been a lie, General," Eleazer began. "Gehazi had not been sent to ask for gifts. There were no young novices visiting Elisha's house. The servant's greed and lust for money brought him here. He hid the gifts when he got back and lied to his master when asked where he had been." He waited for the news to sink in before going on. "The prophet had been given a vision and actually saw you going out to meet Gehazi, General. He saw you giving the man the gifts—so he knew his servant had lied."

"Can this be so?" Naaman exclaimed. "We have all seen the power of God in this man Elisha. How could his own servant think he could get away with such a thing?"

"That is not all, General," Ilani said.

"No, that is not all, my Lord," Eleazer continued. His manner became more subdued. "I remember Elisha's exact words. He said, he pronounced a curse on the servant. He said, 'Naaman's leprosy will cling to you and your descendants forever.'"

Naaman jumped up. "What? What did he mean?"

"I saw Gehazi running away from the house, General. He almost knocked me over. The leprosy of your left arm is now on Gehazi's left arm. His shoulder, and even his face—all bear the marks you had and more appeared white on his skin as he ran away."

Naaman sat back down and shook his head in disbelief. "What a horrible punishment, even for a thief."

"And because the General's gifts had been intended for the man of God, it makes it even worse," Eleazer reminded them.

"The sad, evil man," Naaman whispered.

"General," Ishme said. "Someone's coming." They looked toward the road and in the fading light saw Caleb, Elisha's gardener, walking toward them. He was leading a donkey carrying two pouches hanging over its sides.

"Excuse me, Masters," Caleb said timidly, approaching their camp. "Lord Elisha has sent me to return your money. He told me to tell you to use it for good. That's all he said."

Naaman walked over to the donkey and looked in the two large pouches and found the silver. "He's a man of his word, your master, my friend," he said. "You'll have some supper with us, sleep by the fire tonight and go back in the morning. The roads are unsafe at night."

"I would be grateful," Caleb said.

"Good. Ishme," he called out. "Help this man settle in."

"We will help him," Captain Eleazer said.

"Excellent," Naaman said. "Now what's for supper? I'm starving."

"Our hunters haven't returned yet, General," Ishme said.

Later that night, fresh quail and wild hare were prepared, and enjoyed with several wineskins Eleazer's men had purchased. After the meal, the men built a large bonfire, and men of both armies sat together like a band of brothers. Caleb, the only stranger among them, became their source of entertainment for the evening. Knowing the gardener could tell many stories about the mysterious man of God, they asked him to share them.

Naaman spoke for everyone. "Tell us about some of the other miracles your master has performed."

"I'm not a good storyteller, General, but I'll try. I'll tell you about a couple who lived in the village of Shunem. They were well-to-do and they often invited Elisha to their house for a meal."

Caleb looked around at the men who had stretched out on the ground to listen.

"This couple knew Elisha to be a man of God so they decided to build a small guest room for him. He would be able to stay there, you see, whenever he passed through their village," Caleb explained.

"Well, this touched the prophet so much he asked Gehazi what he could do for the woman, to thank her for her kindness. Gehazi didn't know how to respond at first, then he said, 'I know she has no son, and her husband is old.'"

Caleb looked at the fire, then his listeners and saw he had them in the palm of his hand.

"Go on," Naaman encouraged.

"The prophet spoke to the woman and said, 'About this time next year, you will hold a son in your arms.' And the woman couldn't believe it of course. But as surely as the sun rises, at the exact same time the next year, she gave birth to a son, just as Elisha had prophesied."

"Ahh," the soldiers said, pleased with the story.

"But there's more, my friends," Caleb said. "The boy grew, and one day called out to his father that his head hurt. The father shouted to the servants, 'Carry him to his mother.' The boy sat on the mother's lap until mid-day and then he died."

"Ohh," the soldiers murmured, shocked by the sudden sad turn of his tale.

Caleb paused a moment, and then continued. "The mother carried her son up and laid him on the bed in the prophet's little room, then shut the door and went out. She called to her husband, "Send me one of the servants and a donkey so I can go to the man of God and bring him here."

"The Shunammite lady set out immediately for Mount Carmel where she knew Elisha would be ministering. You see, she believed that somehow the prophet could once again do the impossible. When she drew near, she fell at Elisha's feet, grabbing them and holding on. 'She is in bitter distress,' the prophet said, 'but the Lord has hidden it from me and has not told me why.' Then the woman told him everything. At the end she said, 'I will not leave you until you do something.' So Elisha stood and followed her."

By then, the men around the campfire weren't making a sound. Only the pop of an occasional log in the fire broke the silence.

"When Elisha reached the house," Caleb said," the boy lay dead on the prophet's bed. He went in, shut the door and prayed to the Lord. Then he got on the bed and lay upon the boy, mouth-to-mouth, eye-to-eye, hands to hands. As he stretched himself out upon him, the boy's body grew warm."

Surprised murmuring from his listeners pleased the gardener, and he continued. "Elisha stood and walked back and forth in the small room for a while and then got on the bed and stretched out over the boy once more. The boy sneezed seven times and opened his eyes."

The soldiers shouted and clapped their hands.

"Elisha summoned his servant Gehazi and told him to bring the boy's mother. When she came, Elisha said, 'Mother, here is your son.' She fell at the prophet's feet and bowed to the ground. Then, she embraced her son and held the boy, weeping tears of joy."

There were smiles now on his listeners' faces. Caleb added, "The Lord God uses my master for great good. Blessed be the Name of the Lord."

"May His Name be blessed," the Israelites repeated fervently. The men gathered around the gardener and thanked him for the story.

When he found himself alone with Naaman, Caleb said, "I don't understand Gehazi. He has seen the boy brought back to life, and then you, Lord Naaman, healed from a living death. How could he defy the Lord God Almighty? How could he do it?"

"There is no doubt, Caleb, that Elisha is a man of God who is being used by Him," Naaman said. "Gehazi lived with him every day and knew all about God's power, why would he doubt? For him to be cursed now is sad and tragic, and I'm sorry for him. It tells me I must remain faithful and never doubt—ever." The last words were loud forceful and full of conviction.

"May the Lord help us," Caleb said. Goodnight, General."

"Rest well," Naaman said.

Ishme came to Naaman a little later as they were about to turn in. "Let's head for home at first light, General."

"Agreed. I'm sure Eleazer will be glad to be rid of us.

"I don't know," Ishme replied. "He told me that ever since the first day we crossed the Jordan, these have been the most exciting days of his life!"

CHAPTER NINE

DEPARTURE

As his warriors were washing the next morning, Naaman asked his Israelite host, "Are you sure we shouldn't say farewell to the king, Captain?"

"No, General," Eleazer said. "It would make him more nervous about you than he already is."

Naaman smiled. "I'll follow your advice."

The two groups of soldiers left camp early that day and followed the shepherd's trail they had used before down to the river. The Syrians offered to hunt for game and the former enemies shared a pleasant last meal together.

Eleazer shouted with a grin to Naaman's archers, "Remember—no wild boar!" The Syrians learned a few days earlier that pork could not be eaten.

"I must also begin to observe the Sabbath, if I am to obey the laws of Moses," Naaman said.

"I wish you good fortune with that, my brother," Eleazer said. "It is not always possible for a soldier to rest on the seventh day."

"Nevertheless, I will try," Naaman said.

When the hunters returned with three fat geese, everyone helped clean and dress them before broiling them over the fire. Soon the men were talking about their past few days together.

"None of us will ever forget what happened to you here, General," Eleazer said.

"Nor will I forget the kindness of my enemy—a kindness we did not deserve. I will do all I can to convince my king that our raids on your villages must stop."

"Then our meeting will not have been in vain, my Lord. We too must convince our king to do the same. He will not agree, but we will try."

Both parties made their farewells like old friends.

"Maybe one day when there is peace, you can come and visit my family in Damascus," Naaman said.

"I hope it will be so," Eleazer said. "I would especially like to meet your wife and the amazing servant girl who made it all possible."

Naaman smiled. "Ah, Meira. Perhaps she'll want to come home to her own people now."

"Then tell her she must come to Samaria to meet me," Eleazer said. "My family will make her welcome as will Elisha I'm sure."

"I'll remember, friend. *Shalom*," Naaman called to him as he drove his chariot down into the shallow river.

"And may peace go with you, my friend," Eleazer shouted back. The Israelites rode part of the way up the path then turned and watched as the Syrians reached the other side of the Jordan.

"I grew to like that Israelite," Ishme said.

"As did I," Naaman said. "All of them—I liked everyone we met. Well, all but Gehazi I guess." They still cringed at the mention of his name.

Following the road that ran north and east along the river, they reached the old settlement of Jabesh where they purchased bread and a skin of wine for their evening meal.

"No one seems surprised to find us so far from Damascus," Ishme said.

"Well, by our chariot and horses' saddles they know who we are," Naaman said. "I'm just surprised they are letting us pass."

"Our men are in a good mood. They're glad to be going home."

"I'll never forget what you five men have done for me, brother. I have decided to make our four warriors part of my personal staff."

"They'll be pleased, as am I," Ishme replied. "I know your friend the king will be glad to have you back."

"I hope so. We've been gone a month and that's plenty of time for a lot of intrigue to happen at court. I don't trust the king's advisors. They're always conspiring and trying to advance themselves."

Ishme grinned. "Almost as bad as the army."

That made Naaman laugh.

As night fell, they were close to the Yarmuk River, and set up camp in a grassy area. Releasing Naaman's horses from the chariot they tethered the animals to small trees for the night.

"Guard duty should be two awake while the other three sleep. Do you agree?"

"Yes, General," Ishme said. He was quiet a moment then added, "I recommend tomorrow we sell the iron box as well as the new clothes. We'll conceal the silver in leather saddlebags. I also think we should sell the cart."

"Very well. When we reach the settlement across the Yarmuk, we'll do as you suggest."

"Good. I only hope our precautions will prove unnecessary."

"Better safe. . ." Naaman said. He let his aide finish the rest of the proverb.

The night passed without incident, and in the morning Kala and Samsi said that the only creatures stirring that night were a couple of vipers and a badger. They continued north and reached the river by mid-morning. Several merchant caravans were there, filling their waterskins before heading west toward the Great Sea. The cart sold easily as did the new clothes and iron box. They traded for larger saddlebags and by the time they crossed the river on the small ferry, they felt better prepared for the journey ahead.

Naaman knew his identity had to remain secret, so they told anyone who asked that they were returning to Damascus. They encountered more travelers on the road as they neared Mount Hermon where the main road branched off east toward Damascus.

That evening they set up camp in a small wooded grove and Kala and Samsi went ahead to hunt for supper. The donkeys carrying the sacred earth had proven to be more manageable than they had thought. The animals only needed rest and time to graze along the road.

After a long period of time Ishme said, "Our men should have been back by now."

"I agree," Naaman said. "You and Kapu should go see what's keeping them."

A short while later Naaman watched as Ishme and Kapu returned with the bodies of their missing comrades. The sight sickened him. Both had been killed by arrows. The shafts had been broken off, but Ishme kept their fletchings.

Ishme had trouble controlling his anger. "They're Assyrian, General." He showed Naaman the feathers. "I thought all of Shalmaneser's men had returned to their own country after the war."

"As did I, Captain," Naaman said.

"I regret having to bury them here, General. So close and yet so far from home."

Ilani and Kapu told the officers they would take care of their comrades' bodies. They dug their graves in the shade of a small forest of oak trees. The General said words over their final resting place, and mounds of stones were placed over each fallen warrior.

"We need to leave these woods now," Ishme said. "We're exposed to archers hiding in trees. I suggest we leave now in the dark. There's still enough moonlight for us to see."

Naaman wasn't convinced. The trees provided necessary cover. "Why show ourselves on the road, Ishme?"

"Because whoever did this will not expect us to move at night. They're probably looking for our campfire even as we speak, General."

Ilani knew he would get in trouble for speaking, but spoke up anyway. "Why not fool them and head for the coast, General? We could go to Tyre and then follow the main road to back tDamascus the long way round?"

"That's foolish, soldier," Ishme growled.

"Let him speak," Naaman ordered.

"They'll expect us to be on this road, Captain, but we'd fool them completely."

"He's right," Naaman said. "We could go back in a direction they wouldn't anticipate. We can talk about it later, but let's leave this place."

They mounted up, Ilani and Kapu tying the reins of the riderless horses behind theirs, and Ishme did the same with the donkeys. They rode as far as the crossroad, then turned west toward the Great Sea.

"It's amazing," Captain Ishme said. It was the first time he had seen the ocean—such a large body of water with no land in sight. Only Naaman had been to the coast so the rest of them were in awe of the Great Sea. They were approaching the city of Tyre where they could join with other travelers going east to Damascus. The well-traveled highway along the coast carried people from many nations. Each night, the four Syrians camped away from other travelers to be safe.

The night before entering Tyre, Naaman and Ishme took the first watch. Ishme whittled on a piece of wood while Naaman concentrated on any movement on the highway. The watch changed in the middle of the night, allowing everyone some sleep.

The next day, as soon as they entered Tyre, they met a battalion of soldiers from the Damascus command, easily identified by their shields. An officer rode toward them and quickly dismounted.

The soldier knelt on one knee and saluted. Naaman could see the surprise on the officer's face. "Greetings, General Naaman. We are honored to find you here."

Naaman felt relieved to be back with his own troops. "Thank you, Captain." he said. "Are you commander of this battalion?"

"Yes, my Lord. I am Nadin. We've just arrived in Tyre to escort home the king's ambassador to Egypt."

"This is Captain Ishme," Naaman said casually, introducing his aide, "and the men of my staff. "

"It is an honor, Captain," Nadin replied. "We are headed for the garrison, Sir. Would you care to join us for the mid-day meal?"

"Gladly," Naaman said.

Nadin remounted his horse and led the small party over to his men who were still in formation. When he introduced the general, the men snapped to attention and saluted him with a shout and arms extended straight out in front of them. Naaman drove his chariot beside Captain Nadin, while Ishme rode in front of the warriors. Ilani and Kapu rode at the rear with the donkeys and the two spare horses.

At the barracks, they shared a pleasant meal and Naaman relaxed in the officers' mess with the two captains.

"We had heard you were very ill, General," Nadin said.

"It is true, Captain. But I have been cured by the God of Israel, our enemy. It's a long story and I'll tell you about it one day."

"That is good news, my Lord. You are a legend among the men. But if I may ask, why come this way to go home?"

"We were journeying north from the Jordan River valley, and were attacked by Shalmaneser's renegades. I lost two good men," Naaman said. His voice had started to tremble with anger. "They were in the forest hunting our supper and were shot dead. There can be no doubt about their arrow markings. Therefore we chose the safer road."

"By the gods," Nadin exclaimed. "We had heard there were still bands of Assyrians up in these hills, but have never encountered them. You are fortunate indeed."

"I will ask your superior to give us five or six of your men to accompany the general back to Damascus, Captain," Ishme said.

"General Naaman *is* my superior officer, Captain," Nadin said with a grin. "I'll do whatever he commands."

Naaman laughed. "Well done. When we reach Damascus, I'll bring back another whole regiment to rid this land of Shalmaneser's assassins."

"As you command," Nadin said.

"We are carrying two talents of silver in our saddle bags, as well as some sacred earth on the donkeys. Your men will assure us of a much safer journey, and I will be grateful as will his majesty. Archers would be the best escort possible if you can spare a few."

"I'll see to it myself, General," Nadin said.

Naaman nodded in approval. Later, after Naaman had met with all the men in Nadin's command, the small party left for Damascus with reinforcements.

The road took them up through the foothills of the Atlas Mountains, where the rocky terrain and higher elevation also provided many places for an ambush.

That afternoon, Ishme rode alongside Naaman. "These are good men Nadin has given us, my friend. I may be prejudiced, but Syrian soldiers are better than Shalmaneser's any day."

Ishme grinned. "You're not prejudiced, General. You're simply stating a fact,"

Life became easier for Naaman's small party. The archers found plenty of game in the hills, and having more men to stand watch at night made for a more restful journey. They ate well, and the new soldiers laughed and joked, happy to be escorting the king's Right Hand. In the evening around the fire, the younger men asked Naaman to share stories about battles he had fought and to tell them about life at court.

On the first two nights he told them some of the skirmishes he had been in with King Hadadezer and Captain Ishme. His conscience troubled him, however, because he wanted to share with them the great miracle God had given him, but he hesitated.

One evening as they shared a meal of venison and wine he spoke to his aide. "Should I tell them about Elisha, Ishme?" he asked. "And my illness?"

"With all due respect, General, you had something worse than an illness. The gods gave you a death sentence, and the God of Elisha gave your life back to you. It is up to you, my friend, but it's too great a miracle not to share. You'll have to tell the king in the end anyway, won't you?"

Naaman nodded and fell silent. Looking his friend in the eye he said, "Of course, and you're right. I might as well practice before I have to tell him." That night when asked for a story, Naaman told them what had happened to him. He showed them the new skin growing on his arm and shoulder and they were awestruck.

"Is this some kind of trick?" one soldier asked. "You're trying to see if we'll believe this story or not?"

"No, it's the truth," Naaman replied. "Ask Ilani or Kapu—they were there when I washed in the river. Ask them."

"How can we believe it, my Lord General," another said. "We worship Rimmon, Syria's god and deliverer. Now you speak of a powerful foreign god who leads our enemy. It defies belief."

"As you will," Naaman said. "Ask the king and my family about it—and my regiment in Damascus. I became a leper condemned to die, but look at me now. How do *you* explain it?"

None of them could answer. They simply shook their heads.

The next evening, Captain Ishme told the men about a battle he fought with the general during the invasion of Shalmaneser's army. Naaman's personal story was forgotten, never mentioned again. But the soldiers from Sidon treated him with fear and respect.

Two days out of Damascus, they encountered a Syrian patrol heading their way. The men cheered when they saw Naaman in his chariot.

"May Rimmon be praised," their sergeant exclaimed. The soldiers would have rushed around him if the sergeant hadn't kept them in line.

"Thank you Sergeant," Naaman said. "Carry on."

Ishme said, "That sergeant has sent a rider into the city, General, to let them know you are coming." Naaman frowned but his aide said, "It's too late to call him back. I'm afraid you're in for a happy welcome when you reach the gates tomorrow."

"So much for quietly reuniting with Adorina and the family," Naaman said.

That evening, the men asked about the king and life at court once again, and their general didn't disappoint them. He spoke of Hadadezer's bravery in battle and his strong support of the army. "He treats us as family," he added, "and has our interests always in his head and heart." The soldiers clapped at that and asked more questions until Ishme finally said the men needed to sleep and ordered the watchmen to take their positions.

The small party reached the city gates the next day just as the sun stood directly overhead. A crowd had gathered, and as Naaman led the way into the capital the people clapped and shouted his name.

A younger officer met him, saluted and rode behind him. "His majesty is waiting for you on the palace steps, General."

Naaman nodded, and drove his chariot toward the palace. The crowds on each side of the main road continued to grow, and by the time they reached the palace, the press of people slowed them down. He could see their majesties standing at the top of the stairs. Naaman reined in his horses, then dismounted. Ishme, Kapu and Ilani and the rest of the company stood at attention and watched their leader climb the steps.

"Naaman," the king shouted. "Let us look at you. May the gods be praised. It is good to see you restored to us." To the general's surprise, Hadadezer embraced him. Naaman bowed to the queen and felt overwhelmed by this reception in front of all the people. The king turned him around, took his left hand and raised their two hands together high in the air. The people burst out with shouts and applause.

"Go to your home, good friend," the king commanded. "When you are ready, come and tell us about this great miracle we've heard about. I can't believe it, yet I see it with my own eyes. You are restored." Patting his friend on the back, he encouraged Naaman to go back down the steps alone to shouts of his name which echoed through the narrow streets of Damascus.

The king's Right Hand stood on the bottom steps and small children rushed forward and threw garlands of flowers over him. Naaman caught some and placed the flowers around his neck. Walking toward his men he stepped back into his chariot. Waving to their majesties, he turned his horses around and waited for his men to catch up.

"Take your men to the garrison," Naaman ordered the soldiers who had joined him at Tyre. Turning to his three companions he said, "Let's go home."

CHAPTER TEN

HOME

Outside Naaman's villa, an excited little boy waited by the garden entrance.

"I can see him, Mother," little Ashur shouted. "Papa's coming." He hung on to the front gate of the fence around the house.

Adorina held her daughter in her arms as she stood beside him, her heart beating so fast she thought it would burst. Meira stood close to her. She had heard her servant pray for Naaman every day he had been gone.

"Look Mistress. He's riding with his men. He *is* healed!"

The two women heard the great roar that went up from their neighbors who saw the general driving his chariot toward the house. Some children threw cut flowers on the road while others clapped their hands and danced about. People knew the general had been very sick and had gone to a foreign country for a cure.

Adorina waited patiently as her husband jumped down from his chariot and handed the reins to Captain Ishme. He greeted his neighbors, many of whom had run all the way from the palace to greet him. He thanked them for coming to welcome him home.

Turning to Ishme he said, "After the crowds have gone, you and your men come inside for a supper celebration."

His aide nodded and the warriors remained on the road outside the villa's fence, waiting for the people to disperse.

"My Dearest," Naaman said, embracing Adorina and kissing her gently on the lips. "My Son," he shouted, grabbing Ashur and holding him up to look at him. "Look how he's grown! You must be feeding him lions and bears" The boy started laughing and gave his father a great hug. "Look at my beautiful Atalia," Naaman said, taking his daughter from his wife's arms and kissing her on the cheek before handing her back.

As they walked toward the front door he saw Meira standing by the fence. Walking over to her he took her hand. "I owe you my life, dear friend. I bring words for you from the prophet Elisha, the man of God."

Meira's eyes misted over. "May the Lord be praised," she said.

"Blessed be His Name," Naaman recited, knowing he would surprise her with the appropriate response. Her eyes sparkled as she returned to the kitchen.

Inside, when the door closed, Adorina asked, "Are you truly healed, husband?"

He nodded, removing his tunic and blouse. "Look, Beloved. My arm is no longer covered with lesions, and see my shoulder," turning around so she could see, "and my back as well. The God of Elisha washed it all away."

Adorina could see the tears in her husband's eyes. She handed Atalia to Meira who had joined them, and then embraced Naaman for a long time. Touching his arm she said, "It's so smooth, like a baby's skin." She examined his shoulder and back and couldn't believe her eyes.

"I'll tell you more about it later," Naaman said, "but right now I want to hear from little Lord Ashur." He tickled his son's ribs and picked him up upside down which caused happy laughter and protests from the boy. Putting him down again, he then held his daughter for a long time. His wife smiled. For an instant, it seemed to her that Naaman had never been away.

Adorina invited her husband's men inside for supper. They shared a few of the more amusing stories that happened to them on their month's journey. Later, when the men left and the children were in bed, Adorina invited Meira to join them in the front room.

When they had seated themselves, Naaman began. "I bring greetings to you from Elisha, my friends. He mentioned you too Meira, by name, and admires you for your courage and faithfulness to your God, who has now become my God." He stood and took something from one of his travel bags. He handed her the scroll Elisha had given him. "Elisha gave me a copy of the Laws of Moses. It is a gift to help me learn your faith. He made me promise to share them with you."

He saw his servant's eyes glisten. She said, "There are many of my people who cannot read and who do not have the writings of Moses. But, I do know how to read, Lord General. When my brothers learned, I watched and listened. My mother insisted I learn to read and write. The prophet has given us both a great honor."

Naaman sat down. "Now I want to tell you about the miracle. I call it Meira's miracle." He saw the smile on his servant's face, and began to tell his story. When he got to the seventh time he plunged into the Jordan, Adorina and Meira were barely breathing. Acting it out, Naaman jumped up from his chair and rubbed his left arm and shoulder. "The lesions were gone—washed away, just as the man of God said it would happen." He admitted to being angry at first when the prophet refused to come out and meet him, and again when he required him to wash in the muddy water. "But the Lord was teaching me about humility, obedience, and faith."

"May His Name be blessed," Meira said.

"Let it be so," Naaman answered. He could tell his wife had been over-whelmed by his story.

Adorina said, "What you have told us shows the hand of Israel's God on you since you left."

Naaman nodded. "The prophet loved the meaning of your name, Meira. He said the people of Israel should be like you—bringers of light into a dark and evil world."

Lady Adorina said, "Husband, we've noticed the donkeys. What is in those sacks you've brought home?"

"Sacred earth from the home of Elisha, my dear. I have been conflicted about all of the requirements of this new faith. I thought if I brought this soil, I could stand on it when I pray. I hope it will bring me closer to the God of Israel." He paused a moment, then added, "King Hadadezer expects me as his Right Hand, to continue going to the temple of Rimmon, I know that. But I cannot worship there. You must pray for me, Meira, that the Lord will teach me what to do."

He saw their puzzled expressions, but continued once again. "That isn't the end of the story, my friends." He went on to tell them about Gehazi and his fate. The women were so shocked when he told them what happened to the prophet's servant. For moment no one could speak.

"What a horrible punishment," Adorina whispered. "The poor man."

"But he broke two of our commandments, my Lady," Meira said. "You should not steal, and you should not covet."

Naaman paused a moment, not knowing how to say what he wanted to say. "I have thought long and hard about this new religion and have decided to become a son of Abraham, and my household will follow the Laws of Moses. This will mean the seventh day will be a day of rest. Meira, can teach us more about it."

"Gladly my Lord," the young woman replied. "But are you certain of this?"

"Yes, I'm determined to honor my God."

"It will mean your house must become a religiously clean house, and only those foods allowed by the Laws can be prepared and eaten from now on. It is not something to do lightly. It takes a lot of work."

Naaman noticed the alarm on his wife's face concerning changes to the household routine, so he wanted to reassure her.

"We will do so gradually, Beloved. You and the kitchen staff can work with Meira to make an easy transition to our new way of life."

"As you wish, Husband," Adorina said. She bowed her head politely.

Later, when they were alone in their bedchamber, Adorina said, "I'm so glad you've come back to me, my General." He laughed because she always used his title affectionately, knowing how much he liked it. "I would have died a thousand deaths if you hadn't been healed."

He moved closer and their two bodies fit together as if made for each other. "And I would have preferred to die than to know you could no longer be mine," he whispered. Their intimate expressions of love became a celebration of life itself.

The next morning as Naaman and his wife began their morning meal together, their steward, interrupted them. "Captain Ishme is in the foyer, my Lord."

"Invite him in." The servant nodded.

The captain entered the dining room and nodded politely to Lady Adorina. "Are you ready General?"

"In a minute, my friend." He kissed his wife on the forehead and left to put on his uniform tunic and helmet.

When he came back, Naaman followed his friend outside. The steward brought his horse, knowing the general preferred riding the stallion rather than take his chariot. Naaman greeted Kapu and Ilani who were waiting for him.

"Good morning, General," Ilani said, greeting him.

"A good day you ruffians." He grinned as he got on his horse and led them toward the palace.

As they rode along, Ishme said, "There is something you should know, General."

"What is it?" .

"While we were gone, his majesty put General Irishum in your place. Your friends say it is only temporary."

"What?" Naaman pulled up on his horses' reins. "I can't believe it. He promised he would wait for my return. And Irishum of all commanders? I can't believe it. He's a capable leader of course. When did you learn of this?"

"When we returned to our barracks last night," Ishme said. "It's no secret. Everyone knows. What can you do about it, General?"

Naaman gently kicked his heels into his horse's flank and urged the animal forward again. "There's nothing I can do, really," he answered. "The position of the king's Right Hand is given at the king's pleasure."

"Yes," Ishme grumbled, "but I think it's wrong for the king to have done this."

"Let it be, Captain," Naaman said. His tone became suddenly official. "My loyalty—*our* loyalty is to the king." He had a hard time keeping his disappointment out of his voice.

"Yes, Sir, as you say."

When they neared the steps of the palace, the royal guards took charge of their horses, and the two officers climbed the granite steps and went in. A servant invited them to be seated in the reception hallway and ran to find the Lord Chamberlain.

"Something's not right," Naaman said. Under his breath he added, "I've never been made to wait. Ever."

"Perhaps there is a council meeting," Ishme said.

"All the more reason to admit me at once. I'm part of the king's council." His voice became louder and Ishme had to pull on his arm to calm him. Suddenly General Irishum stood in front of them. Naaman frowned as they stood and saluted.

"Ah, Naaman," he said. He did not refer to his colleague's rank or position. "His Majesty is occupied for the moment and I'm afraid you'll have to come back later. He did not know you were coming this morning."

"Irishum. I might have known you would take advantage of my absence. I will speak to His Majesty about this."

The general grinned. "I don't think so. All audiences with His Majesty must be approved by me."

Naaman turned to leave, but stopped. "The poor man. To have as his Right Hand the man who almost let him die in our last battle."

Irishum put his hand on the scabbard of his sword, but that's all. His face turned red but he did nothing.

"Let's go, Captain," Naaman said. "There a bad stench in the palace!"

That evening as Adorina served a delicious supper to her husband and his aides, someone knocked loudly at the outside door.

Their steward ran to it and returned quickly. "It's Lord Mardokh, General."

"Show the Chamberlain into the front room. I'll come at once," Naaman said. Looking at his friends he said, "Wait here, I'll come and tell you what he wanted after he leaves."

Meira drew the curtain across the opening to the dining area when her master left.

"Lord Mardokh, this is a great honor," Naaman said. "Have you already eaten? You are welcome to join us."

"Thank you, General, but I've come on an important matter."

"Let's go into the garden," Naaman suggested. He led the way outside. When they were seated and an oil lamp brought, Naaman asked, "Now what is it old friend?"

The elderly courtier cleared his throat. "About a week after we learned of your affliction and you had gone for a cure, General Irishum answered a summons to the palace. He and the king met privately several times, which I learned about afterwards. Hadadezer believed you would not and could not be healed. Therefore the next most senior officer should be made his Right Hand—and so he named Irishum."

"I see," Naaman said. "I must say I'm saddened and disappointed that his majesty did not keep his promise." The general stood and removed his tunic showing the Chamberlain where the lesions had been.

Mardokh said, "It is indeed a miracle. You *are* whole again. Let the gods be praised."

"Even so," Naaman said. He decided not to argue about which god had been responsible for the miracle.

"I come tonight, General, not only because of Irishum, but because of what he is pushing the king to do." Naaman became apprehensive. "He's asking for a declaration of war against Israel and is already planning an attack."

"The Lord help us," Naaman said. "It will be a disaster, my Lord. Israel has the most powerful God in all the world on their side. He's been defeated by their God before, Lord Chamberlain. I am living proof that He can conquer the most deadly of diseases. I understand he has also raised the dead. Syria will not stand a chance against Him."

"Then you must warn the king, my son. He is your friend and always listens to you."

Naaman nodded. "But how? Irishum has locked the king in a box."

"Give me a private invitation for his majesty to come to your house for a meal in two days. I will personally give it to him," the elderly man vowed. "I know the king, and if he decides to do something, he'll do it—no matter who tries to control him."

"Yes, excellent," Naaman said. He called for his steward who rushed into the garden. "Bring my writing materials and parchment." The servant hurried back into the house and returned with them, placing them on a flat thin board.

"Let me do it, General," Mardokh said. "I've had more practice and can write faster than you."

"Good, carry on," Naaman said. When the chamberlain finished, Naaman signed it and added a personal note: 'From him who still has the scar from the sycamore tree.' He smiled because he knew only the king would know the letter came from Hadadezer's childhood companion. "Tell Lady Adorina to come and bid my guest goodnight," he told the steward. The servant bowed and carried the writing materials back inside.

When Naaman and the elderly man reached the front room, his wife met them and bowed her head to the nobleman. "Good night, Lord Chamberlain. You have done us honor by your visit."

"Good night, dear Lady," Mardokh said cordially. "May the gods bless your family this night and all nights to come."

"Good night, Lord Mardokh," Naaman said, placing his hand on the statesman's shoulder. "I shall not forget this kindness." When he had gone, his three friends came into the front room.

"I have some bad news, friends," Naaman said. He told them what he had learned and how the king would be coming to supper in two days. "I rely on you, Adorina, to make it the best meal you can serve him."

"It will be as you say, Husband," she said.

"But it would be foolish for us to attack Israel now, General," Ishme said scowling. "Foolishness."

Kapu added, "With the God of Israel on their side, it would be a disaster."

"I agree," Naaman said. "That's what I tried to tell the chamberlain." He paused for a moment, then added, "Ishme, I need you and your men to gather all the information you can about how our men in the ranks feel about Irishum. I'll need it before I meet with the king."

"As you command," Ishme said.

"Good, rest well tonight. And remember, keep my meeting with the king a secret. We wouldn't want Irishum to learn of it." His men saluted, and after bidding good night to Adorina, left the villa.

Husband and wife walked together to their children's rooms and looked in on baby Atalia, and then little Ashur, who lay spread-eagled across his bed. Naaman eased him under the covers and they kissed their son good night.

As they prepared for bed, Adorina said, "It will be a lot of work to get the king's meal ready." She was brushing her hair, something Naaman liked to watch her do.

"But if anyone knows how to please 'Dezer and the queen, it is you," Naaman said. "Just prepare the feast as you always do when they come."

"Why would he replace you with that vile Irishum? What a beast of a man."

Naaman laughed, but knew his wife had described the man perfectly. "Irishum comes from a poor family and has no patience with people at court or anyone who he considers rich or well off. We don't know why the king has done this, my Love. That's why I want the king to come for supper. I hope he'll be honest with me. I have to think of some way of keeping the general and his cronies away from the king that night."

"You've had a lot of discouraging news today, my Lord Husband," she said. She moved away from her dressing table and pulled the covers back on her side of the large bed. The oil lamp was extinguished, and she opened the curtains to let in the moonlight.

As he lay down on the bed, she turned toward him and said, "That's why I waited until now to tell you this. Your God of Israel has granted us another miracle. I am with child once more." Naaman let out a shout and embraced her. They laughed and kissed, then laughed some more.

"We are blessed by the Lord God," Naaman said.

"It is so," Adorina whispered. She leaned closer and kissed him passionately.

CHAPTER ELEVEN

HADADEZER

On the day of the king's planned visit, a chariot arrived at Naaman's villa, escorted by four guardsmen on horseback. The general and Lady Adorina had only just entered the dining room for their morning meal.

As soon as Naaman heard them arrive, he knew something was wrong, and called for his steward. "When I have gone with these men, get word quickly to Ishme and my men. Tell them to come for me and do all they can to release me."

Suddenly a loud pounding on the front door demanded immediate attention and Darius ran to answer it.

The officer who had driven the chariot said, "We have come for General Naaman on the king's business!"

Naaman went to the door. "Tell me the king's order," he demanded.

"You are to come with us without question, General," the officer said.

"Very well," Naaman replied. "Your name, Captain?"

"I am Shakra, General."

"Darius," the general called to his steward. "Bring my horse."

"There is no need, General, you'll ride with me," Shakra said. It was more of an order than a suggestion.

"I'll be going to General Irishum's, Darius," Naaman told his steward matter-of-factly.

"Very good my Lord," Darius replied. The five guards looked at each other in surprise.

Naaman smiled, pleased to show them he knew who they were.

"Enough," Shakra said. "We must go at once."

Naaman walked to the chariot and stepped in. He didn't think Irishum would try anything this soon, but now the king's new Right Hand had made his choice. Naaman held on to the railing next to the captain, his feet planted firmly on the platform as Shakra drove out of the city.

Naaman knew this was Irishum's first mistake because his men would know where to find him. He only prayed that a large number of his battalion were still loyal.

When they pulled up in front of the general's villa, Irishum came out to greet him. "Well, well, Naaman! I'm so pleased you have decided to accept my invitation for supper. You'll have to excuse the early hour. Captain Shakra has always been a little too anxious."

"Like his commander, I imagine," Naaman growled. He stepped down from the chariot and stood in front of his rival. "His majesty will not be pleased by this."

Irishum feigned surprise, "His majesty? Why, the king has given me a free hand to help him in matters of the military. I've simply invited a colleague to my house for a friendly supper." Turning to Shakra he said, "Escort him inside."

The captain nodded, took the shortsword from Naaman's belt, and pushed him toward the front door. Once inside, other guards tied his hands behind him and forced him to sit in a chair.

"You'll have to forgive me, foreigner," Irishum said. There was an increasing menace in his voice. "That's what you've become now isn't it? A traitor loyal to Israel?" He waited for a response but when Naaman didn't answer he went on. "I couldn't let you meet with the king as you planned. Two boyhood friends getting together, no, no, you might still influence him. I've put a stop to your supper plans."

Naaman spoke in a cold voice. "Is the army yours to command now, Irishum? Are you sure all the regiments will follow you?"

"Of course. They've been told what a leprous deserter you are," Irishum said. "I don't know if I should even allow you in my house." He walked over to his prisoner and tore Naaman's tunic and blouse from him. He looked carefully at the man's body then said, "Well, you've been cured anyway—there can be no doubt of that."

"A God bigger than Rimmon or all our gods has healed me, Irishum," Naaman said. "I would be afraid of keeping *me* prisoner if I were you."

Irishum slapped Naaman hard across the face. "I'm leaving," he told his men. "Guard the prisoner and when I return I'll decide his fate. You are in charge, Captain."

"Yes, General," Shakra said.

Naaman heard Irishum drive the chariot away and prayed Ishme would be able to convince his men to come to his rescue.

Captain Ishme saw Naaman's steward running toward him out of breath. When Darius told him Naaman's instructions, Ishme couldn't believe it. "What do you mean?"

"They've taken him Captain, to General Irishum's villa. He orders you to come for him."

"Ilani," Ishme shouted. When the soldier came running he ordered, "Assemble the men at once."

Ilani ran to the barracks and assembled the men of their battalion in front of the buildings.

Ishme faced the soldiers who stood at attention. "Men, Irishum has arrested our General, and taken him to his villa. I want two-man patrols to go find out what's going on. One will go to the palace, and the other will reconnoiter Irishum's villa. Find out what you can. Carry your swords, but make no attempt to engage anyone. You are on a fact-finding mission and that's all. Return quickly and we'll reassemble here—is that understood?"

His men nodded and saluted.

Ishme turned to his aides. "Kapu and Ilani, you remain here," Ishme added. "That's all men, dismissed." Ishme could hear the angry buzz sweeping through the ranks as the men talked about the abduction of their general. In Ishme's small office, Naaman's three friends put their heads together.

Ilani shook his head. "If he's at the palace dungeon, there's little we can do."

"True, but he's probably at a secret location," Ishme said. "I don't think Irishum is really foolish enough to hide the general at his own residence. On the other hand, he *might* be that sure of himself."

"If he's at the house, we overpower the guards and set him free," Kapu growled. .

"If he's at Irishum's, that means he's done this without the king's knowledge or approval," Ishme said. "If Hadadezer had approved, they would have taken him right to the palace dungeon."

"They'll have sentries at the villa, Captain," Ilani added. "Our archers can pick them off. Getting inside will be more difficult."

"True," Ishme said. "We could force our way in from every side, but they'd kill the general before we could reach him."

"What if we burn them out?" Kapu asked.

Ilani didn't like the idea, but Ishme stopped him.

"No, it's a valid tactic—the only problem would be how to save the general. Irishum's men would probably leave him there to die." He saw the concern on his subordinate's faces and stopped to think some more. "In any case, we'll wait until we know more. Our men should be back soon. Why don't you two go and see what you can learn over at Irishum's barracks."

"Good idea," Ilani said. He and Kapu left, heading toward the other side of camp.

Within a short time, the men sent to reconnoiter returned with their reports.

"They're not holding him at the palace," the first two announced. "General Irishum's there, and according to the palace guards, he should be there all day."

"General Naaman is at the villa," the second team reported. "We saw two guards leading him outside to the latrine and his hands were tied. He seemed all right from what we could tell. There were six guards who rotated inside and outside during the short time we were there. Their horses are behind the villa."

Ilani and Kapu returned and told Ishme that Irishim's warriors were relaxing and were not preparing for anything special.

"Excellent," Ishme said. "Now assemble the men and we'll plan a course of action."

The regiment reassembled and Ishme told them how the rescue would take place. Speaking in a loud voice, he said, "The key is secrecy, men. Eight of you will block the road leading in and out of the villa. Word must not reach Irishum at the palace."

"I need twenty archers," he continued. "The second unit told me the archers will be able to pick off the guards outside. Another team will have to rush inside from behind the house through the garden. If there is a dog, kill it to avoid detection. The life of our General is at stake—remember that. Those chosen to enter the villa must charge in with swords drawn. Save the servants if you can, but if they're in the way, don't hesitate to kill them."

"I can only take fifty of you with me. Volunteers step forward." He had to smile when the whole regiment took a step forward. "All right—we'll decide by drawing numbers."

With the fifty selected, Ishme chose eight men for the road barricade and the twenty archers. The rest would enter with him through Irishum's garden. They would have to go on foot. "This must be done as fast and as quietly as we can. We'll go in different directions and wait for my signal." Everyone nodded and he ordered, "Move out."

The eight soldiers for the road went first, followed by the archers a few minutes later, then Ishme's men headed into the hills in order to swing around behind the general's villa.

"May Naaman's God be with us," Ilani whispered.

"Even so," Kapu answered.

The lack of circulation in Naaman's hands was painful. He struggled against the ropes to try to give himself some relief. At least they had untied his feet so he could walk outside to relieve himself. He tried to imagine what his men were doing. They would first have to block the road and circle the villa. He prayed to the Lord God to help him, feeling guilty asking for His help again so soon.

From his chair, Naaman could see out the front windows. His heart beat faster at the sight of several small puffs of dust blowing up with the breeze. Something had moved near the house. It could be wild hares or pheasants. He watched Captain Shakra standing outside, looking down the road. Suddenly a look of shock appeared on his face as Naaman saw an arrow burst through his chest. He died instantly. Naaman heard the impact of other arrows hitting their targets around the house.

Before the two guards inside could kill their prisoner, archers rushed into the house from the back and quickly cut them down. Ishme and Ilani ran to Naaman's side.

"What took you so long," Naaman said as Ilani cut through the general's ropes. "The Lord be praised! "Good work, men. Good work."

His soldiers rushed into the house to see him. He patted each of them on the shoulder and thanked them personally. "Any casualties, Captain?"

"None my Lord." He grinned. "Well, unless you count Kapu cutting his hand with his own sword" Everyone laughed except Kapu who turned red, and hid his hand behind his back.

Naaman suddenly became silent and his men quieted down. "I have a supper to go to. His majesty is expected at my house at sunset and I must prepare for his visit."

"Use their horses, General," Ishme told him. As his men saddled the animals, Ishme asked, "But how do you know his majesty will come tonight? Surely Irishum has told the king you won't be there."

Naaman thought before answering. "You must take another letter to him, Ishme. I'll write it in my own hand which he'll recognize. Take it to Lord Mardokh. He's a good friend and will make sure it reaches the king. Try not to be seen, of course."

"As you command, General," his aide replied. He and Naaman took two horses and rode off, leaving the rest of the regiment to remove any evidence of them being there and to remove the bodies. They took the dead men up into the hills behind the house. The soldiers forced Irishum's servants to walk back to the barracks with them. Naaman smiled, because when General Irishum returned home he would find his house empty and no trace of what had happened.

The letter to King Hadadezer suggested the king not leave the palace until after General Irishum had gone home. Naaman included words and phrases only Naaman and the king would know. He wanted to be sure the king knew he had sent it.

That evening, Naaman greeted the king and queen at his home. "Welcome Your Majesties."

Adorina stood beside her husband as the royals stepped down from their chariots. Queen Atalia and Adorina embraced, and then went inside. Their husbands followed behind. In the front room they sat down and shared conversation.

"General Irishum gave me the impression that you wouldn't be here tonight, Naaman. Why would he say that?" the king asked.

Naaman thought quickly. He had always been honest with his friend. "He said it because he arrested me this morning and took me as his prisoner. I've been tied up at his villa all morning."

"Gods,"The king shouted angrily. "Explain yourself"

"It's true, Majesty,"Adorina said. "We were about to sit down to our morning meal when his soldiers burst into the house and took my husband away."

"My dear," the queen said, suddenly frightened.

"Why would he do this without my approval?"

Naaman could see by the frown on the king's face he was displeased by these revelations. He cleared his throat and looked his friend in the eye. "You made him your Right Hand, Dezer. That's why. He thinks he can do whatever he wants in your name. He would have killed me tonight when he arrived home."

"No! I can't believe it," the king protested. "You are a member of my court, Naaman. He wouldn't dare."

"Yes, old friend, he would. He considers me a traitor because I went to Israel for help."

"A traitor?" the king said. "Certainly not. You of all people."

In a kinder tone, Naaman tried to explain. "He believes because of my leprosy, I went to Israel to be cured. You lost confidence in me and pushed me aside. Therefore I had to be disloyal in some way—and a traitor, Majesty."

Queen Atalia interrupted her husband. "Perhaps you have misspoken, General. You imply the king has deliberately made a mistake."

Naaman heard the warning in her words and immediately corrected himself. "What I meant, Great One, is that when I found it necessary to leave your side, you needed someone in my place. You couldn't have known Irishum would be so treacherous."

"Even so. I will handle this, my friends," the king said. "You have always been my Right Hand and I should have remembered that."

Queen Atalia changed the subject hoping to calm the men down. "Tell us what happened on your journey, Naaman?"

"I will, Great Lady. I'll gladly tell you everything."

After the sumptuous meal, the two couples settled on the cushioned divans in the front room. Naaman amazed the royals with his story. The king asked to see where the prophet healed him. He was astonished to find Naaman's perfectly healed skin, and the places where the lesions had been so visible when the two men met at the royal farm.

"Then *their* God really and truly *is* God?" Hadadezer asked.

"He is, my Lord. He has raised the dead and cured many of their illnesses through the intervention of his prophet Elisha."

"I see," his friend mused.

"May I see little Atalia?" the queen asked suddenly about her namesake.

"Of course, Majesty," Adorina replied. "In fact we wanted to use this occasion to make an important announcement."

"Oh?" the king said.

"Yes, Naaman's God has blessed us, Majesty. I am once more with child."

"My dear friend!" the queen exclaimed. "How wonderful for you both."

"Congratulations, you old fox!" the king said. He pounded his friend on the back.

"Come, Majesty," Adorina said beckoning to the queen. "We can tuck Atalia in together."

When the women came back, Meira came with them. Naaman heard the queen say, "You truly saved your master's life, Meira."

"It was my duty, Majesty," Meira said. She bowing her head courteously to the queen. "When you have the light, you must share it with those who are still in darkness."

Naaman winced, knowing the young woman hadn't realized she had just insulted the national religion.

Naaman asked the king, "What will you do with Irishum, Majesty? He tried to kill me."

"Tell me how you escaped, brother," the king asked.

"My men surrounded his villa and dispatched his men easily. Expertly done."

"Then you have taken away his power, Naaman. I will send him far enough away so he can do no further harm. To execute him would only incur the wrath of his battalions—something I will not do. I need a united army." He saw his friend nodding in agreement. "He'll be sent to Tyre to maintain our western frontier."

"I've just come from Tyre, Highness," Naaman said. "There are good men there, and the general's troops can bring much needed reinforcement in the fight against the bandits who seem to be growing in numbers. Your decision is a wise one, Majesty."

The king grinned. "Thank you, General. I expect you back on the council tomorrow as the king's Right Hand."

"You honor me once more, Majesty," Naaman said. "I will not fail you."

"Besides," the king added. "If this prophet helped you once, maybe he'll be willing to help you again."

"Only if it is his God's will, Great One," Naaman said. "The God of Israel cannot be manipulated by us or anyone."

Hadadezer became thoughtful after that for some time. Naaman became afraid he may have offended him. "Do you no longer believe in Rimmon, the god of your own people?" the king asked.

Naaman immediately recognized the danger in the question but answered anyway. "Rimmon could not heal me, Majesty. Only the God of Elisha could do that. I therefore choose to worship his God and learn His ways."

"Your people will not understand," the king said. "This is an important matter, and when we can meet with the priests, we'll look into it carefully." The two couples made their farewells and Naaman watched as the king and queen rode back to the palace.

As she kissed him goodnight, Adorina asked, "Did my supper succeed, Husband?"

"Their majesties were pleased, and that's all that mattered, Beloved." He stretched out on their bed and added, "I only hope Dezer has learned he can trust me more than before."

Adorina sighed. "I know he is your friend, Naaman, but you could have died today because of the king's choices. Don't trust him."

CHAPTER TWELVE

CHARIOTS OF FIRE

A month later, King Hadadezer called a special council meeting. When Naaman arrived, he took Lord Mardokh aside. "What is this about?"

"He's going to ask the army to begin raiding Israel again, General. "Some of us are opposed, but we're in the minority."

"I knew this recurring proposal would come up again, but I didn't think it would be so soon, Naaman said.

The old man nodded and took his place at the large table.

When the king arrived, everyone stood until his majesty was seated. Naaman noticed immediately that his friend wouldn't look him in the eye—a bad sign.

"Gentlemen," Hadadezer began, "As you know, we are constantly harassed along our border with Israel. I am ordering the army to send in soldiers again to punish King Joram's renegade militants."

Naaman spoke up. "The army is ready to obey, Majesty. But will this not lead us into war?" He looked directly at the king as he said it.

"Perhaps a war is what we need, General," the king said. "Israel must be defeated once and for all."

"As you command, Majesty," Naaman said. His response surprised many on the council.

"Good! Set up our camp near the city of Dan in the north, General," the king ordered. "We can send regiments across the border from there."

"Agreed, Great One, we can leave in the morning if you're ready."

"I'm ready Naaman for you to lead the way," the king said.

Naaman stood and saluted. The councilors realized it would be useless to discuss the matter with the king since he had already made up his mind.

In Samaria, the capital of Israel, King Joram's steward rushed into the royal apartment out of breath. "The prophet is outside, Majesty."

The king scowled, unhappy with the news. "Bring him to me out on the veranda." He hurried into his chamber to change clothes.

Afterward, the king greeted Elisha outside in the shade of the date palms. "How may we help you, Voice of God?"

"It is I who can help you, my Lord King," the older man said.

"I see," Joram said. Of course he had no idea what Elisha meant. "May we offer you some wine?"

Elisha sat down on a granite bench, not waiting for the king to sit first. He shook his head. "No, thank you. I've received a vision and a warning, my king."

Joram's stomach tightened into a knot and he swallowed hard. He received warnings before, but chose to ignore them. "Go on," the king said.

"I saw in my vision your enemy coming to invade the kingdom, King Joram. This time, the king of Syria will be at Dan and his attack will come from there. You must send soldiers there immediately to thwart his plans."

"You say you can see and hear the king, my Lord. What does that mean? Do you have spies in Syria now?" He could see by the frown on the prophet's face, the older man didn't like the impertinent question.

"Majesty, I am called a 'Seer' for a very particular reason. It means the Lord lets me 'see' and hear things that will affect you and the country. You can be assured that this is the word of the Lord." The prophet stood, intending to leave.

"Wait, don't go, Elisha," Joram insisted. He stood. "Tell me more."

"There's nothing else, Majesty. Do as I have told you and you will prevent more suffering for your people." Elisha didn't wait for permission, but turned and left the king's presence.

Joram walked to the hallway just outside his residence and called for one of his guards. "Send for General Eleazer at once," he commanded.

Naaman and his battalion set up camp near the Israelite border. Entering the king's pavilion he stood at attention, waiting to be recognized. He was bringing bad news.

"Are we ready, General?" Hadadezer asked. He motioned for him to sit down.

Naaman looked around the king's tent trying to find the words to tell his friend what he had discovered. "No Great One, we are not ready. There are Israelite patrols all around us. I don't know how it happened, but it's as if they knew in advance where we would be setting up our command post."

"It's not possible," the king shouted. "How could they have known?"

Naaman didn't have an answer and only shrugged his shoulders. "I'll ride out and try to discover what is happening, my Lord. I'll return as quickly as I can."

The king nodded, dismissing him.

Naaman took Ishme, Kapu and Ilani with him. They moved closer to the Israelite camp outside the town of Dan and hid in a small wooded area.

"We need to get closer," Ishme said.

"Maybe when it's dark," Naaman replied. "They must know we've already seen them. I fear they are in larger numbers than I anticipated. It's as if they were prepared for this."

"Let Kapu and me go in tonight, General," Ilani said.

"Agreed," Naaman mumbled.

Returning to camp, Naaman told the king they would try to infiltrate the enemy camp, but Hadadezer didn't respond, continuing to stare off into space.

When Naaman returned to his men he said, "The king's not a happy man."

"It seems Elisha's God is looking out for his chosen people," Ishme said.

"I've thought of that too," Naaman added.

Later, hearing a sound high above him, Naaman watched a skein of geese flying in formation, outlined against the pale gold and coppery tones of the western sky. His warriors started fires throughout the camp and the four friends slipped away to the woods between the armies. When the Israelite camp settled for the night, Kapu and Ilani removed their outer tunics and spread dirt on their skin. They pushed through the brush and trees, heading toward the enemy camp. They were gone for what seemed a long time. Suddenly, a movement in the tall grass revealed his men, but instead of two, there were three.

"Eleazer!" Naaman exclaimed when he saw the familiar face. Then he put his hand over his mouth for fear of making too much noise. The two officers greeted each other with enthusiasm.

"It is good to see you my friend," Naaman began. "Why are you here?"

"I could ask you the same thing, General," Eleazer replied. "Elisha told our king you were coming. More specifically, that you were coming to Dan. The Lord warned him."

"Ishme and I both believe this is the Lord's doing," Naaman said. "We know it. I will tell my king we must leave here. I will do all I can to avoid a confrontation."

"As will I," Eleazer responded. "We must keep the armies apart."

"Let it be so. Say nothing to your men about our meeting, but you can be assured we will leave here."

"It was good to see you again, my brother. Have you truly become a son of Abraham?" the Israelite asked.

"Yes, as soon as I arrived home," Naaman said. "My household now follows the Laws of Moses. Tell Elisha this if you ever seen him again, Captain."

"It's General now," Eleazer said. He couldn't stop a grin from spreading across his face. "I will do as you say." Turning around, he saluted the Syrians and disappeared into the darkness.

Walking back to camp, Naaman said, "The king's not going to like this."

The frustrated Syrian king moved his camp to Rabbah, but by the time they arrived, the Israelites were already there waiting for him. He then moved to a clearing near Beth-shean, only to find his enemy there too.

Naaman became alarmed. He didn't know if he would be able to control the king's anger. Hadadezer might foolishly decide to attack the enemy without giving thought to any plan.

"This is three times, Naaman," the king shouted. He had called his general to the pavilion. "Can you tell me who the traitor is? Someone is telling the Israelites what we are doing. I want you to find him and bring him to me."

"I already know and will tell you, Great King," Naaman said." You won't believe me, so you must calm yourself and listen."

"Very well," Hadadezer said. He forced himself to be seated.

Naaman took a deep breath. "There is no traitor here, Majesty. It is Elisha the prophet who is doing this. He tells your enemy, the king of Israel every word you utter in this tent."

"Bah, that's impossible and you know it."

"Not so, Majesty," Naaman said. "He is a seer, remember? I told you how he knew beforehand that his servant would come to me for money. Remember that story? He was able to 'see' it happening. He is able to connect, through the power of God, with people's minds." He paused to let the king reflect on his words. "He's doing it now with you, Dezer. He knows what you are planning."

The king jumped up. "How is this possible? We've not told anyone else our plans. Only you and I have known and you've been with me all the time." He paced about the tent for a few minutes then stopped and shocked Naaman with his next words. "Find this Elisha," the king ordered. "I'll send men to capture him."

"But Majesty," Naaman protested. "If he is a servant of the all-powerful God, wouldn't you be putting the army in great danger?" He recognized the scowl on the king's face and knew his friend wouldn't change his mind.

"Do as I say, General. Bring this prophet to me."

Naaman saluted and left the tent with his heart in his throat. He must save God's servant somehow, but how?

Israel's prophet walked along a dusty country road. The young man at his side shook his head and asked, "But why Dothan, Master?"

Elisha smiled at his young apprentice. "I do not question the Lord's directions, Shallum. You should know by now that the ways of the Lord are not our ways. We listen and then obey."

"Yes my Lord," Shallum mumbled. They were approaching the gates of the ancient village. The prophet explained to him that Dothan existed long before the time of the Patriarch Joseph and the other fathers of their nation. Even though it was an ordinary town, it was nestled in hills of lush green grass, and became a favorite gathering place for shepherds.

Elisha knew the Syrians were trying to find him, yet he entered the village square without alarm. The people began clapping and shouting his name. To them it was an honor when God's Spokesman came to their town. They would take good care of him. That first evening, a room above the old inn provided a respite for the two visitors. As soon as Shallum's head hit the pillow, he began snoring, making his mentor smile.

The man of God walked to the only window in the room. As he looked up at the sky, he could see what he thought were clouds forming in the distance, but as they came closer he recognized what they were. Walking back to his simple cot, he lay down again and fell asleep.

When Shallum awoke the next morning, he took a pail outside to draw water. Something bright caught his eye as he pulled up the pail. The object in the sky shimmered in his eyes and reflected the morning sun. As he rubbed them, he realized the light came from the reflection of hundreds of gleaming swords and helmets. Dropping the pail, he ran back inside, and raced up the stairs.

"Master!" he shouted. "The enemy has us surrounded. There are soldiers everywhere with horses and chariots. What shall we do?" Shallum fell onto the floor trembling.

Elisha moved toward the window and saw the Syrians encircling the city and simply smiled. "Don't be afraid," he told the young man. "Those who are with us are more than those who are with them." He could see by the doubtful look on the lad's face that he didn't believe his master's words.

Elisha covered his head and lifted his hands to the Lord in prayer. "O Lord," he prayed, "open Shallum's eyes so he may see." The apprentice stood and followed Elisha outside to the village square. The army of Syrians was plainly visible from there.

Suddenly, Shallum shouted, pointing to the sky, "Oh my. Can you see them, Master? There are thousands of horses and chariots of fire in the sky hovering above the enemy. It is the Lord," and the young man fell onto his knees.

"He is to be praised indeed," Elisha said. "Wait here, my son." To the apprentice's horror the man of God walked out through the city gates and headed for the advancing Syrian army. As the enemy came down toward him, Elisha lifted his hands again and prayed once more to the Lord.

"Strike these men with blindness, My Lord!" Suddenly, beginning with the front row of soldiers, the Syrians stumbled forward, throwing their arms out to stop their fall.

"I can't see," men cried out. At the very moment of Elisha's prayer, the Syrian army became blind.

Shallum rushed to his master's side. "Be careful, Master," he said. "They might still strike out and kill you."

Instead, Elisha went up to the man he could see to be an officer sitting on his horse. "My Lord," he said, "you are on the wrong road, and this is not the city you seek. Follow me and I will lead you to the man you are looking for."

The officer, so confused by his blindness, didn't respond at first. "It must be a sandstorm that has blocked our sight," he cried. Turning his head back toward his men he shouted, "There is someone here who has offered to lead us to the prophet. Follow the sound of my voice."

"It's only a few leagues away, my Lord," Elisha said. "Do you want to go there?"

"Yes," the soldier replied. "We are on a mission for the king. Lead on."

"Then I will guide you."

The Syrian shouted orders to his battalion and everyone stumbled forward, following the voice of the stranger.

In Syria during this time, the king, Naaman and his war council, returned to Damascus.

"It won't take an entire army to arrest one man," the king bragged to Naaman. "You must remain here in the capital with your men in case I need you."

Naaman saluted and returned to his men. He waited outside the city walls with the king's guardsmen, dreading the moment he would learn of Elisha's capture.

"It's not right," he told Ishme. "Why send a whole battalion to arrest a holy man?"

"Agreed," his friend said. "I would hope the Israelite king has sent enough soldiers to protect him."

"Elisha would not accept help," Naaman said. "He believes His God is enough for him. The Lord will protect Him."

"He's always been right," Ishme said.

As they waited for news, the guards helped villagers from the towns around Damascus come into the city in case of attack. Shortly after the sun reached its mid-point, a rider raced up the dusty road toward the city.

"It's a farmer," Kapu shouted. It soon became evident the man came from the fields. He rode bareback and his tunic, torn and ragged, dripped mud. When he reached the soldiers, he jumped down, falling onto the ground out of breath.

"Our soldiers have been captured, my Lords," he managed to gasp between breaths.

"Who, my man?" Naaman shouted.

"The whole army. A neighbor rode over to tell me and I rode through the night!" He stopped to catch his breath again. "There is an old man leading our soldiers away."

"What?" Naaman asked. "Are you sure?"

"Yes, my Lord," the farmer said. "Our men have been struck blind! All of them. There is a holy man leading them away to Samaria!"

"By the gods!" Kapu shouted. He paused and placed his hand over his mouth. Apparently surprised by the words that came out. "Sorry, General. My old habits are hard to forget!"

Naaman, totally shocked by the news, knew it must be true. It could be the greatest victory King Joram would ever win. The mighty Syrian army defeated by one man—the holy prophet of Israel.

"Let's prepare, Captain," Naaman ordered. "Tell his Majesty we must raise the defenses of the city in case the Israelites decide to attack the capital." Naaman felt sorry for the man. He would have to deliver those words to Hadadezer.

After giving the exhausted man some water, Ishme asked, "How far do they have to go?"

"They could be in Samaria before the sun sets, my Lord, but remember, they're blind and are not surefooted."

"Our king will not be pleased by such news, my friend," Naaman told the man. "Stay here with my aides. It will be safer for you. His majesty has a violent temper."

As the man gulped down the water, he shook his head. "I must go right back."

Naaman took his aide aside. "He's done it again, Ishme! We've been afraid we'd have to fight our Israelite friends on the battlefield. Elisha has worked it all out for us."

"It will be a massacre though, General," Ishme said. "When our men reach the capital they will be put to the sword. Now blind, they won't be able to defend themselves."

"A sad day for us, indeed," Naaman replied soberly. "Imagine the king's reaction when he learns his army won't be coming back, and that he has lost Israel's secret weapon."

CHAPTER THIRTEEN

LEADING THE BLIND

At the king's palace in Samaria, General Eleazer stood on the veranda next to the captain of the guards. Suddenly he saw a puff of dust kicked up by something on the road below. He shouted, "There's a rider coming, Majesty. I'll find out who it is."

King Joram came to the railing and saw the dust. "It could be nothing," he grumbled.

"I'll go to the gate, Great King," Eleazer said. He hurried out of the king's apartment and ran down the steps to the city gates.

When the rider came closer, Eleazer could see he was dressed as a merchant or wealthy villager. The general's men stopped him when he reached the entrance to the palace.

"Let him pass," Eleazer ordered. The man, perhaps in his twenties was covered in sweat and dust. "Give him water," the general said. A soldier brought a waterskin. When the man had drunk his fill, he sat down and looked up at the general.

"They're coming this way," he began. "A whole army of Syrians, my Lord."

"Syrians? The Lord help us," Eleazer said. "Sound the alarm, call the archers to the walls.".

"No, no, my Lord," the man protested. "Elisha is leading them and they are all blind and can't see a thing."

"Blind?" Eleazer asked. .

"Yes sir. One of their officers is on his horse and is being led by the man of God."

"How far away are they?"

"Still about half a day," the man replied.

"Wait here. The king will want to reward you."

"Thank you," the rider replied, bowing his head.

By the time the general made it back to the king's veranda, he too, had to catch his breath.

"It must be bad news if you've run all the way up here," Joram growled. I'm not sure I want to hear it."

"The Syrian army is on its way here, my Lord King. Don't be alarmed. It is not an attack. The Lord God has made them all blind and Elisha is bringing them to you."

"By my father's beard!" Joram swore. "Can it be true?"

"I believe the man, Majesty. He looks like a merchant and has nothing to gain by lying."

"Of course, General," Joram said. In a serious voice he asked, "What do you recommend we do?"

"Majesty. I'll call our soldiers to stand with their weapons at the ready once the enemy is inside our walls."

"Do so at once."

Eleazer saluted and left again.

"What do you mean, blind?" one of the general's aides, asked. "What did that fellow mean, General?"

"We don't know, Joshua," Eleazer answered, "But if Elisha is leading these men then the Lord is responsible for it." The general began to worry about his friend Naaman. If he was among these blinded warriors, he wouldn't stand a chance of defending himself. He added, "A soldier always prays for an honorable death—fighting with sword in hand. It will not be possible for these Syrians."

"Send Aziza to find out where they are," Eleazer ordered.

When he was found, he mounted and rode out at a gallop to locate the enemy. The sun had reached its highest point when Aziza returned and dismounted.

"They're almost a league away, General. They are about to reach the tall sycamore. It is true about Elisha. He's walking in front of them with his servant, leading the officer's horse. I'm sure they'll need to stop at Nathan's Spring for water."

"And this blindness? What about it?" Eleazer asked.

"They're eyes are open, General, but they can't see anything. I saw them tripping over rocks and holes in the road. It is no ruse—they truly are blind."

Eleazer nodded. "How many are there?"

"I calculated by regiment and believe it's at least three thousand, maybe more."

"Good work," Eleazer replied, dismissing him. The soldier nodded and went to join his comrades.

General Eleazer returned to the palace. The king and royal family had come onto the veranda.

"They're almost to Nathan's Spring, Majesty. One of my men has returned to say they are about three thousand in number."

"Three thousand?" We'll *have* to kill them now. That's too many prisoners to handle," Joram said. "I did not imagine there would be so many."

"Nor I, my King," Eleazer said. "Perhaps the man of God will have an order from the Lord as to the fate of these men."

"Elisha? Why, Elisha, General?" Joram exclaimed. "Is he King of Israel now? No. Elisha will not have the final word about how we treat the enemy."

On the dusty road, the blind Syrian captain asked, "Are you sure this is the way?"

Elisha didn't look back at the man on the horse but said, "Yes my Lord. There is only one road that leads to the town you're looking for."

"We must find water," the officer said.

"Yes, in fact a little further along there is a spring. Your men can drink and rest for a while."

"Good. Why are you being so kind to us?"

"Let us just say I am a servant of my God who does what he is told," Elisha answered.

Shallum smiled at his master's answer.

"I understand," the Syrian responded. "But it is unreasonable to expect to be treated so by one's enemy."

"The God of Israel doesn't think as we men think, Captain. His ways are beyond ours." They reached the spring and Elisha said, "Ah, here we are. You'll have to use your hands to bring the water to your mouth. I'll try to help your men." As the officer dismounted, Elisha led him to the water. Each man helped the next and it took them a good while until everyone had drunk enough.

"We'll have to move a little faster, my Lord," Elisha told the officer once he was back on his horse. "We want to arrive before the sun goes down."

"I heard a rider come by a while ago," the captain said.

"Just a curious onlooker," Elisha replied. "Such a large number of soldiers is always cause for alarm in my country. He rode off as soon as he saw who you were. My people still fear you."

"And so they should," the officer said.

Elisha frowned at his boasting bravado. The Syrians were soldiers unable to fight.

When they were back on the road, Elisha's aide suddenly said, "There it is, Master! I see the town!"

"Good," Elisha said, "we'll be there in plenty of time."

"The man we are seeking doesn't know we're coming," the officer told them. "He will undoubtedly run away when he sees us approach his village—an army of blind men."

Elisha smiled. "Oh he'll still be there, Captain. He'll be there."

Inside Samaria, Eleazer shouted up to the royal family. "Here they come." Those in the palace rushed to the edge of the railing and watched the great cloud of dust approaching the city.

"Come down Majesty, and meet your enemy. I don't know how he did it, but Elisha has brought them to you."

"Yes, he most certainly has won a victory," Joram grumbled.

Eleazer saw the frown on the king's face and knew it didn't please him to admit it. He waited while the king reached the city square, surrounded by his palace guard.

"Let them enter, Majesty. We'll subdue them once inside," the general said.

"Of course, Eleazer. I'm no fool," the king growled.

There were no inhabitants to cheer or applaud as Elisha and his servant led the unsuspecting Syrians through the city gates. When the prophet saw the last row of soldiers enter, he motioned for the gates to close.

Eleazer watched in amazement as Elisha pulled his tallit over his head and lifted his hands in prayer. "Lord, open the eyes of these men so they may see." The Lord answered his prayer immediately.

The Syrians felt something and began rubbing their eyes. They couldn't open them very far because of the bright light.

"I can see," one soldier shouted, soon joined by hundreds of others. When they could see each other again they began laughing and pounding their comrades on the back.

"By the gods," another shouted. "Look." Suddenly they realized they were inside the fortress of Samaria, surrounded by Israelites whose swords and bows were drawn.

"I am the man you seek, Captain," the prophet revealed to the officer he had been leading. "I am the prophet Elisha. But do not fear." He left the astonished officer and walked toward the king. He bowed his head and waited for Joram to speak.

"What is the Lord's will, my Father? Can I destroy them now?" The king asked.

Elisha was surprised by the king's question, and every Israelite looked to Elisha for a response. "No, you will not kill them, King Joram. Set food and water before them so they may eat and drink and then allow them to return to their master." Not waiting for the king to respond, the prophet of God turned around and walked back to the Syrians.

"Sit down where you are," he told them. "You will not be harmed in any way. Instead, our king will have water and food brought to you. You are safe inside our capital city." When he finished speaking, Shallum repeated his words to all the soldiers down the line.

Eleazer couldn't believe what was happening.

The captain of the Syrian army followed Elisha and said, "My Lord, a word please. Is this true? Will your king do what you said?"

"He will, Syrian. He is not in command here. It is the Lord God of Israel who commands him. Now be patient. It will take a while to prepare your food."

The captain's mouth hung open in disbelief.

King Joram became angry. He insisted Eleazer walk back to the palace with him. When they were back in the king's apartment he shouted again. "I'm not going to do this. Elisha can't make me do it."

The general didn't correct him. The man of God could strike the king dead or blind, but he chose not to remind the king of it. "You must do as he says, my King. His words come from the Lord."

Joram slammed his fist down on a table. "But have you ever heard of such a thing? In all our years of history no king has ever acted so cowardly."

With the king's pride at stake, Eleazer knew he had to answer carefully. "Great One," he began. "No one has heard of a king being so magnanimous with his enemies. It is a merciful and honorable way to treat a defeated enemy. It is a victory achieved without the shedding of a single drop of blood. What other king has done such a noble thing?" Eleazer hoped his words were beginning to have an effect.

Joram sat down and began to pull on his goatee. "It is true isn't it? It will be an honorable victory over our old enemy."

"Yes, Majesty and it might even be the beginning of a peace between us.

"Yes, well—that is to be seen," the king growled. "See to the feeding of our prisoners, General. We will watch from here."

Eleazer knew Joram didn't want peace—he wanted to destroy Damascus. He had said so many times in their war councils.

"Majesty," Eleazer replied, saluting. He left the palace and when he reached the square again, he watched the feeding of the prisoners. He never dreamed he would see such a thing and it went against all reason. He found Elisha and his servant sitting on a bench over-seeing it all and he told them of his amazement.

"Why are you so astonished, General?" Elisha said. "Are you so lusty for the blood of these men that you cannot show them mercy?" He watched Eleazer's reaction before continuing. "The Lord our God is a God of mercy. We know in our history how many times we as a people were undeserving, yet He showed us mercy. Now, He is doing the same for an old enemy. We cannot fight the will of the Almighty."

"I don't understand it, my Lord Prophet, but if it is of the Lord I can accept it. The king, however, may not be so merciful."

"When these men have finished their food, they will be allowed to leave and return home, General. It is what the Lord wants."

"Joram will not allow it, my Lord," Eleazer warned.

"I will be the one to tell him, my son. Give it no thought. These men will be set free, and there is nothing he can do about it." Elisha did not speak like a man with doubts.

"Very well, my Lord." He decided not to be there when Elisha told the king. He watched as the old man climbed the steps to the king's apartment. Then, walking around the square Eleazer observed the enemy eating and drinking. Their weapons were confiscated and locked in the armory. The captured soldiers surprised him by not showing any resistance.

As Eleazer approached the Syrian officer in charge, the man stood and nodded to him. "I cannot understand what is happening," the officer said.

"Nor can I, Captain, but none of us can fight Elisha. He is the voice and hands of our God,"

"Will you assure us of an honorable death, my Lord? We have no weapons, but want to die as soldiers."

"You are going to be set free, Captain," Eleazer said. "I've spoken with Elisha and he told me it is the will of our God. You are going to be shown mercy. Your weapons will not be given back, however."

The captain scratched his short beard then shook his head. "We have heard about this prophet—this Elisha. We have been sent to capture him. He healed our greatest general of an incurable illness."

"Naaman, you mean General Naaman," Eleazer exclaimed. "I saw it happen. I saw the Lord heal him. My men and I were his escort. We grew to respect him." .

"By the gods. You know General Naaman. I can't believe it. If I am able to return home I must tell him about you. How are you called, my Lord?"

"I am Eleazer, General of his majesty's army. Give him my greeting, and also Kapu, Ilani, and. . ." he had to pause and think, "oh yes, Samsi and Captain Ishme as well."

"This is unbelievable," the Syrian said, and then, he too, became thoughtful. "In some ways we are alike, as soldiers I mean. Someone tells us what to do and we do it—no matter which king or nation we belong to."

"It's true," the general replied, "We are all at the mercy of our rulers."

"Elisha's coming," one of Eleazer's men shouted to him. Eleazer went to meet the prophet.

"Have the Syrians stand, General. They are free to go."

"And his Majesty, my Lord? My orders come from him after all," the general replied.

"Let them go," the king's voice said behind him,

Eleazer saluted. "Yes, Majesty." He walked over to the officer with whom he had been talking. "Move your men out, Captain. Peace be with you."

Still amazed, the Syrian saluted the king with his arm outstretched, got up onto his horse and spoke to his soldiers. "Move out, men. We are free to go." A great shout went up as the men stood and got in ranks behind their officer.

Eleazer watched something he never believed he would see. Enemy soldiers leaving Israel in peace.

"Good riddance," several of his own men shouted as Eleazer walked back toward the king.

The king frowned. "I hope I'm not going to regret this."

"Now there will be peace," Elisha said. "There is nothing to regret, my son."

"I would not want to be *that* captain when he arrives back home," Eleazer said.

"Nor I," the king replied.

Eleazer smiled at Elisha. "Well, my Lord Prophet, how did it feel to be the subject of a manhunt by the Syrian army?" .

"No different than when you two hunt me down," Elisha said. "You do it all the time." The man of God unsuccessfully tried to hide a grin. "But I'm pleased the enemy raids will stop."

With a puzzled look on his face, the king asked, "How can you know that?" Then he suddenly realized he knew the answer. "Oh, but of course. You see everything *before* it happens don't you?"

"Not everything," Elisha answered. "I'm not the Almighty. I am but His servant."

Shallum approached his master, and the prophet told him they were going home. As the elderly man turned to go, Eleazer said so only he could hear, "The officer told me Naaman and his men are well, my Lord."

"Naaman—ah yes. I am pleased hear it. I remember that stubborn soldier with some affection." He smiled cryptically. "I wonder what he did with all that dirt?" Turning around, he followed his servant out of the palace and headed for home.

CHAPTER FOURTEEN

WINDS OF WAR

Two years passed and Naaman marveled that peace had continued between Damascus and Samaria. General Irishum's forces on the west coast had rid the countryside of thieves and mercenaries, and Naaman's patrols encountered no Israelite raiders along the borders. Still, King Hadadezer was not happy. He became more aggressive at every council meeting and his advisors were concerned he would push Syria into war.

"Can't you convince the king that it would be unwise to attack Samaria, Lord Chamberlain?" Naaman asked Mardokh one evening at supper. Since the elderly man lived alone, Naaman felt sorry for him and invited him to his home once a month. He and Adorina enjoyed his company, as did their children.

"You know the king, my son," Mardokh said. "It is sad that he's fixed on Israel's destruction."

"Yes, my Lord, I thought I knew him. You would think he would look more kindly toward them after King Joram's merciful treatment of our army. He even provided them with food and drink before sending them back. And now, for us to send the same men back to attack the hands that fed them is not right."

Just then, Naaman's son Ashur ran in with his little brother Hadad. The elder statesman had taken a special liking to the boys.

"Forgive me, Father," Ashur said. "We wondered if the Lord Chamberlain wanted to see us." Naaman had to keep from laughing and he and Mardokh grinned at each other.

The chamberlain asked, "What makes you think I'd want to see you two young Lords?"

Ashur smiled. "Because you like playing with our toys too, my Lord."

The nobleman laughed. He never came to supper without bringing something for the three children. Mardokh motioned to his steward, who brought in something covered by a blue linen cloth. He placed it on the table in front of the old man.

"Come here," Mardokh said, and the boys hurried to his side. When he nodded, Ashur removed the cloth and discovered a miniature chariot and carved wooden horse.

"Oh, look," Hadad exclaimed. "The wheels turn and everything. Thank you my Lord." Hadad tried to touch it but Ashur pulled back his little hand.

"An expensive gift my Lord," Lady Adorina said smiling. "You continue to spoil them."

"I know, I know, but please let this old man have some happiness in his life." He helped the boys carry the miniature toys over to the tile floor in the front room. Naaman followed them and sat on the divan, watching his boys pull the horse and chariot along.

"Men never grow up do they?" Meira observed to her mistress as she cleared the table.

"Meira," Naaman responded. "Be kind."

"They never do I'm afraid," Adorina laughed. "But do any of us?"

"My Lady. Of course, we are the mature ones, unlike men."

"Perhaps, but I find myself holding little Atalia's dolls too long sometimes when I'm in her room. I'm so glad she's finally old enough to play with them."

The chamberlain stood and put his hand on Ashur's head. "Enjoy your very own chariot my boy, but remember, the horse is just as important as the driver."

"I will my Lord," the boy said.

"Walk me to my chariot, General, if you don't mind." Naaman sensed some anxiety in his friend's voice. Adorina came to bid their guest farewell and the chamberlain's driver went to bring the chariot to the front door. Mardokh turned to speak to his friend.

"The king doesn't want you to know, but he's going to send General Irishum to lay siege of Samaria. He feels your connection to this man Elisha will affect your ability to command."

"By all that is holy," Naaman exclaimed. "How can he do such a thing after the mercy shown by the people of Samaria? How can he?" He struck his fist into the palm of his other hand in anger. "And why didn't he tell me himself?"

"You'll oppose him and he knows it, my son. You must be careful in the days ahead not to get in his way. I'm an old man and my family are all grown or dead, so he can only harm me. But think of your family, Naaman."

Naaman calmed down. Mardokh had just given him valuable information. As he helped the chamberlain into the chariot, Naaman put his hand on the man's shoulder. "May the God I now serve be with you and protect you my good friend."

"And with you, my son," Mardokh whispered. It sounded almost like a prayer.

Naaman watched the chariot leave, then went back inside. "Darius," he called to his steward. "Go and tell Ishme to come and bring his two aides with him."

"Yes Master," the servant replied.

"Take my horse and be quick about it," Naaman added.

A short time later, when his three friends arrived, he explained to his wife that she shouldn't wait up for him. "We're meeting in the garden on an important matter and I don't know how long it will take." She nodded, knowing he wouldn't come in for a long time.

Ishme and the others didn't speak when Naaman joined them. He brought a garden lamp on a pole and placed it into the ground between the benches.

"Speak quietly, brothers," he explained. "My family is asleep and I especially don't want my wife to hear any of our discussion." The three nodded, waiting patiently for him to tell them why they were there.

"The king has decided to send Irishum to invade Israel," Naaman growled.

Ishme was the first to speak. "Irishum? Why him, my Lord?" Then he suddenly knew the reason and said it out loud, "It's because of you and Elisha, isn't it?"

Naaman nodded. "That's what Mardokh and I believe. He's going to lay siege against Samaria—the very city that showed our soldiers mercy and brought these years of peace."

"Does this mean your battalions will be left behind, General?" Kapu asked.

"I don't know. The chamberlain seems to think the king will tell me once he's made his plans."

"Well, I wouldn't want any part of the siege," Ilani admitted. "With Elisha there, the army will not stand a chance."

Kapu said, "But our men will not be happy if they're left out, General. What will you tell them?"

"Nothing yet Kapu, until I hear from his majesty. I might even suggest the king allow me to retire. We all know he prefers Irishum now. That's why he's sending him in charge of the attack."

"But you're not old enough to retire," Ishme argued.

"Maybe not," Naaman chuckled. "But I'm old enough to know when the king is ready to make a change. I want to keep my head for my family's sake."

"Understood," Ishme said.

"As for you members of my team, I'll make sure you are part of the Royal Guards," Naaman continued. "The king will not refuse my request." His friends smiled at that, and Naaman could see on their faces they were relieved to know he had been thinking about their futures too. "I'll get word to you once I know something. My only worry is for my men. How will they take the news?"

"They'll want to go to Samaria, of course, General," Ishme answered. "But if you explain that we are needed here to defend Damascus from possible attack, they might accept the news with a better attitude."

"The men will think I'm no longer fit to command them in battle."

"Not so, General," Ilani said. "They've seen you in battle and will follow you anywhere. The men with families will be glad they're not going, and so will the rest. They've heard about the power of Elisha and wouldn't want to be blinded or something even worse."

"Thank you," Naaman said. "I don't want to sound unsure of myself, but I've always trusted your opinions. I ask that you not say anything to anyone until I've spoken with the king." His men stood and saluted. Kapu pulled up the lamp pole and carried it back to the veranda. They wished Naaman a good night and left the villa by the side gate.

"Good men," Naaman said under his breath. He entered the front room and walked barefoot down the hall to his bedchamber. He slipped quietly into bed and listened to Adorina's soft breathing before he drifted off to sleep.

In Samaria, Israel's capital, Elisha woke to loud noises on the road near his house. He removed his nightshirt and put on his simple one-piece robe. "What is it?" he shouted to Shallum.

The young man stood just outside the front door. "We're being attacked, my Lord. The Syrians have surrounded the city."

"It's begun—the hunger and death," Elisha said. "They're going to lay siege, my son. The Lord has revealed it to me."

"I'm glad this house is within the city walls, Master."

"Yes, but the only food we'll have is growing within this garden fence, my boy. Pull up what vegetables you can and hide them in a safe place before our neighbors come for them." He thought for a moment and added, "Tie up old Moses next to the house before someone steals him as well. In the coming days people will eat anything, even a donkey."

"Yes, Master. What else can we do, Holy Father?"

"Pray to our Lord for deliverance," the elderly man said.

General Eleazer, Commander of the Israelite Army, stood high on the wall surrounding the fortress city of Samaria. Hundreds of archers were also stationed along the top of the wall. He knew they were no match for the thousands of Syrian warriors camped around the city. Earlier, the Syrians had attacked the surrounding villages, and hundreds of people died outside the walls, unable to reach safety within.

"Aim for their horses, men," the General shouted. "Their chariots will be useless to them."

"As we anticipated, they've camped out of range, General," his aide told him.

"Then save your arrows and energy. Don't fire unless you have a sure target." As Eleazer climbed down the stone steps from the wall, King Joram awaited him in his chariot.

"What are they doing, General?" the king asked.

"Nothing Majesty. They are camped just out of our reach. They're going to starve us out."

"And with all of your soldiers now inside the walls, our food will be gone that much faster," Joram complained.

. Eleazer bit his tongue, stopping himself from saying how selfish the king's remark had been.

"We've also placed men with barrels of water at our city gates, Majesty. The enemy's been firing flaming arrows at the wooden structures, hoping to burn through them. If they succeed, that will be the end. We are outnumbered two to one."

"I don't want to hear these things," Joram growled. "Tell me what you've planned in order to stop their attack."

"Vigilance, Majesty. Our soldiers must watch every moment or their army will get through the wall somewhere. This is only the first week. I can't imagine how long they might camp out there. Thank the Lord we have deep wells."

"The Lord is not helping us," the king said. "Why didn't the prophet blind them again, or rain down fire upon them like his predecessor Elijah did to the priests of Baal? I told you we shouldn't have let those soldiers go. They were in our hands—now see what's happened!"

Eleazer didn't answer because the thought had also troubled him.

By the end of the first month, things became difficult. Grain to make flour was gone and there would be no more bread. All the animals in the capital had been eaten and even pigeons became a feast for those lucky enough to capture one. But as the siege continued into the middle of the fifth month, the people were starving and desperate.

One day when the king walked beside Eleazer on top of the wall, a woman called up to him. "Help me my Lord King."

"If the Lord doesn't help you, woman, how can I help you? There is no food anywhere," he shouted down to her. Both men could see the desperation on her face. The king asked, "What's the matter?"

Pointing to the woman standing next to her she said, "This woman asked me yesterday to give her my son so that we could eat him. 'Tomorrow we will give you our son,' she promised. So we cooked my son and ate him. But today I said to her, 'Give up your son so we may eat him,' but she's hidden him, my king."

Joram, horrified by her words, tore his robes and nearly fell off the wall. A crowd had gathered during the woman's story, and the people looked up and saw the king throwing dust on his head. He was in mourning as if for a member of the family. When he climbed down from the wall, he declared loudly so that everyone could hear, "May the Lord do his worst to me—and even more to Elisha, son of Shaphat. His head will not be upon his shoulders by day's end. General Eleazer, send for the executioner. I want to cut off a head."

"Yes Majesty," Eleazer replied.

Some of the elders of Samaria met in Elisha's nearly empty front room. Very little furniture remained. The man of God and his servant could not even offer the elders anything to drink except water. The men came to plead with the prophet to intercede with the Lord for the deliverance of the city. They came on the same day each week, but Elisha's answer was always the same: "I have not heard from the Lord."

Today, however, he suddenly jumped up. "Hear me," he shouted. "The Lord has revealed something to me." The elders stood, too excited by the good news.

Elisha continued, "Even as I speak, that murderer, King Joram, is coming to cut off my head." His visitors, alarmed by his words, started toward the door.

The prophet called to his apprentice. "Shallum, lock the doors and hold them shut against the king's man. I know the king won't be far behind."

Shallum locked the front, side and back doors. Abruptly, they heard a loud knocking at the front door.

"Open up, Elisha. This is Japheth, the king's Right Hand. His Majesty is right behind me—open the door." The elders began to shake with fear, and Shallum led them out into the back garden where they hid themselves among the bushes.

Elisha stood behind the front door and listened to Japheth's voice. Suddenly, another voice he knew well caused him to open the door. He bowed his head slightly to the king, and Joram and Japheth walked into the room. Elisha smiled, relieved that the king suddenly turned to his executioner and ordered the man away.

The king paced around in the house then asked in an angry loud voice, "Why should I wait any longer for the Lord to answer? I've given up on God." He then sat down on one of the few chairs in the room.

Elisha smiled and remained standing in the center of the room. "Then listen to this, Majesty. Listen to the Word of the Lord. He says the famine is over. At this same time tomorrow, a measure of flour will again sell for only a shekel at the city gate."

Japheth, the king's Right Hand, thought the prophet was mocking the king and said angrily, "Look, even if the Lord were to open the windows of heaven, how could that happen?"

Elisha walked up to the king's man and stared him in the eye. "You will see it with your own eyes, Japheth, but you will not eat any of it."

Outside the gates of Samaria, four dirt-covered beggars lay on the ground. The oldest, Hanun, looked like a skeleton. All his ribs were showing through his crinkled skin. He couldn't remember when he had last eaten.

"Why are we still here, brothers?" he said. In addition to their hunger, the four men were lepers. "Even if we were allowed inside the city, we'd still die of hunger."

Nahush coughed several times. "And if we stay here, we'll die."

With a great deal of effort, Ethan used his crutches to stand. "I say we should go to the Syrian camp and surrender. If they spare us, we'll live; if they kill us, then we die. Death is staring us in the face either way."

"I agree," the fourth man said, nodding his head.

"You always agree with Ethan, Gareb," Hanun snarled. "They'll see what we are and won't let us near their camp." At dusk the four men got up and with what little strength they had, made their way toward the Syrian camp.

"Wait. Listen," Gareb said, stopping on the road. "What is that sound?" The others stopped, and suddenly they felt the ground begin to shake and a strong wind blew toward them.

"It sounds like hundreds of horses riding this way. Get off the road," Ethan shouted. At that moment, several strong gusts blew the four men to the ground.

"Let's go back," Nahush shouted above the noise. The rumbling lasted a long time and the lepers remained crouched down on the side of the road. Ethan's and Hanun's feet, badly ravaged by their leprosy, required them to use crutches to hobble along. They were strongly opposed to going back.

Hanun said, "The sounds are almost gone—let's go." Resuming their journey little by little, they painfully made their way toward what they hoped would be their deliverance.

"Can you see anything, Ethan?" Hanun asked the only one who could walk normally. He was up ahead of them now.

"Nothing yet, brothers," Ethan replied, "I'm almost there."

"I'm not going to make it," Nahush warned his friends. "My arms can't hold me up on these sticks anymore."

"There's a large tent up ahead," Ethan shouted to them. "But someone should have come out and challenged me by now."

His companions tried to move faster but Ethan seemed to disappear, hidden in the cloud of dust up ahead.

"Ethan!" Hanun called out. "Where are you?"

"There's no one here, brothers," Ethan shouted running back towards them. "The enemy camp is empty. They've all gone."

CHAPTER FIFTEEN

HEAVEN'S WINDOW

On the plains of Israel near the Jordan Valley, an officer ran into the Syrian general's tent. He needed a moment to catch his breath.

"General," the aide shouted. He pushed on the officer's shoulder to awaken him.

"Wha? What's happening?" Irishum shouted angrily.

"We're being attacked." His aide handed the general his tunic and helmet. "The Israelites have hired the Hittites and Egyptians to attack us. We must retreat."

Irishum rushed out of his tent and heard the thunder of hoof beats approaching from the southwest. He felt the ground tremble with the vibrations of an army heading his way.

"Sound the retreat. Leave everything and go" he shouted. Across the camp the startled soldiers grabbed their clothes and began running east toward the Jordan River.

"May the gods strangle King Joram in his sleep," Irishum shouted at the night sky.

"Hurry, General, you can't be captured," his aide exclaimed. He held the officer's horse until Irishum had mounted and the Syrian army fled camp, leaving everything behind.

Some distance from the city of Samaria, four lepers entered the Syrian camp hoping to be given scraps of food.

"What do you mean the camp's empty?" Hanun asked.

"Come and see for yourself, brother. There's no one here," Ethan said. He helped his friend walk into the empty tent.

"Look," Gareb shouted, "food." He took a bite of some fresh bread and drank some wine, gulping it down.

"Take it easy," Hanun warned. "A little at a time. Our stomachs must get used to food again."

"Look at the golden handle on this sword," Nahush exclaimed. "And these silver cups and knives."

"Let's take what we can carry and hide it someplace safe," Ethan suggested.

"Good idea," Hanun said. "They might come back at any moment." The four men collected everything from the first tent and carried it to a cache in some rocks on the hillside. Then, they moved on to the next tent.

As they were about to enter, Hanun stopped them. "This isn't right. This should be a day of good news for Israel and we're keeping it to ourselves. If we wait around until morning we'll get caught and punished. We must go and tell King Joram about it."

"Are you mad Hanun?" Ethan grumbled. "These treasures will help us and our families for a long time. We deserve this."

"Do we, Ethan?" Hanun asked. "If the noises we heard a while ago came from the Lord of Heaven, then it is He who has saved our people. He will not be pleased if we keep all this for ourselves, while our people starve to death in the city."

Nahush said, "I agree, brothers. Our people are dying. We must help them." In the end, the four lepers agreed to return to the city. Leaving what they had hidden in their safe place, they took two donkeys for the two men who had trouble walking, and headed back.

Arriving in the middle of the night, the lepers awakened the gatekeepers of Samaria and told them the Syrians had fled. The men didn't believe them at first but finally sent word to General Eleazer.

Keeping his distance from them, the general listed to their story and decided they were telling the truth. He ran to the king's apartment. "Majesty," Eleazer shouted as he ran. "Majesty," He shouted again.

Joram hurried to the door half dressed. "What is it?" he bellowed.

"We believe the Syrians have gone, My King."

"It's not possible." The king spoke first out of surprise, and then disbelief. "Come in General. Sit down." He began to pace up and down in his front room. "I'll tell you what the enemy has done, General. They know we are starving and so they've left the camp and are hiding up in the hills. They figure we'll come out and they'll capture us, finally gaining a way into the city."

Eleazer couldn't believe the king's words. If what the lepers said was true, then the Lord had delivered Samaria once again, and the king couldn't accept it.

Japheth, the king's aide and Right Hand, rushed into the king's apartment and heard the end of the king's words. "You should send some of our men and let them find out what's happened, Majesty."

"A good suggestion, "Eleazer said.

"And you can carry out your idea, Japheth," the king commanded. "You will go."

The king's aide swallowed hard, not expecting he would be the one chosen. "As you command, Majesty," he said.

He and Eleazer left the king's palace and walked down to what had once been the king's stables. All but five of the king's horses had been eaten, and those left were thin and weak.

"I'll help the men get a chariot ready," Eleazer said. "You'll take the best archers with you of course." The young man nodded and Eleazer saw the fear in this eyes. "If this is the Lord's doing, brother, He will go with you."

"I'd rather you were coming with me, General," Japheth said nervously. "I'm not a soldier."

"And so I shall," the officer said. "His majesty doesn't need to know. You can be the one to report to the king when we return." Eleazer smiled when a look of relief passed over the face of the king's aide.

"Thank you, General. I am grateful."

Eleazer nodded and went to select the archers for their mission.

At dawn, two chariots raced through the gates in pursuit of the Syrian army. By midday they returned and reported to the king.

"Majesty," Japheth began, "the enemy has fled across the Jordan and are nowhere in sight." Members of the court and elders of the city who had also rushed into the audience hall to hear the report, shouted for joy and clapped their hands. "Everywhere we found the road strewn with their clothing and equipment—thrown away in their headlong flight. The camp is full of food and plunder ready to be taken, my King. It's all but a short walk away."

"Excellent," Joram said. Turning to Eleazer he asked, "And how should we proceed General?"

"I would put some of my men at the city gates to maintain order, Majesty. Then, let the people go out at dawn. They are starving and there will be very little we can do to maintain order."

"I agree," Joram said. "Lord Japheth, as my Right Hand, I want you at the city gates to supervise those going in and out."

"Yes, Majesty," his said. He was pleased the king had given him an assignment of such importance.

Early the next day, before the sun rose, a great crowd of Samaria's inhabitants waited for the gates to open. Some were pulling carts, while others brought large sacks in which to put whatever they could find. Eleazer's soldiers stood by the gates and opened them slowly, hoping they could maintain some kind of order as the people rushed out.

After only a short time, Eleazer's older sons were first to return with food for the family. As hundreds of other returned, people began to have hope again. At the end of the day the general went to the palace to make his report.

"Tell us what you saw, General," Joram asked. He still refused to show himself to the people for fear their desperation would make him their scapegoat.

"The people have food again, Majesty," Eleazer began. "They've also gone beyond the camp to the farms in the valley. People are sharing their bounty with each other, bringing back all they can carry. For the first time in six months I heard singing again. But the most mysterious thing is the story of the four lepers. They were the men who told us the Syrians had gone during the night. I met their spokesman—his name is Hanun. He said he heard the thundering of horses hooves in the dark. The ground trembled so much it knocked them off their feet. He said it sounded like a great army marching toward the Syrian camp."

Joram grew serious. "Elisha said this would happen, General. He told us in his house the day I went to kill him. He said the famine would end that very night, and that there would be food enough for everyone." He looked around as if trying to find someone, then asked, "Where is Japheth?"

"He was our only casualty, Majesty. The crowd pushed through the gates with such force, they crushed him. A tragic accident."

The king's face suddenly showed fear. "By my father's beard. Elisha said that would also happen. The prophet had not been pleased by one of Japheth's remarks about what God could do. He made fun of the prophet. Now the prophet's words have come true. Elisha is right again."

"For which we should be grateful to the Lord, Majesty," Eleazer said. He was hoping to encourage the king.

"It is true," Joram said. He took hold of his queen's hand. "We *are* grateful."

Eleazer knew from past experience that the king's declaration was insincere.

Back in Damascus, Naaman and his family relaxed in their garden, enjoying the cooling breezes from the river.

Ishme intruded, telling the steward he had important news. "The siege of Samaria is over, General. Word of Irishum's unexpected retreat has already reached Damascus. We've learned from one of the general's aides that the withdrawal was cowardly and dishonorable."

"Irishum may be many things, but I can't believe he is a coward," Naaman said.

"But even his own men believe it to be so," Ishme said.

"What has his majesty done about it?"

"He's thrown the general in the dungeon along with five of his battalion commanders," Ishme reported.

"As you know Ishme, today is the Sabbath. I cannot travel to the palace. Keep me informed about what's happened," Naaman said.

"Of course, my Lord. Excuse the disruption of your holy day." Ishme saluted and left the villa.

Naaman smiled, because his aide had also become a believer in Naaman's God. However, he had not yet accepted all of the changes his new-found faith required.

Returning once more to the tranquility of his garden, Adorina sat beside him on one of the woven divans. As long as the mild weather permitted, the happily married couple passed their Sabbath reading the holy book Elisha had given them. Merira had helped translate it for them. They enjoyed watching their children play until they took their afternoon naps. When Naaman shared with her the news about Irishum, she remained silent a long time.

Naaman finally spoke. "What is it my love?"

"Don't you see, Husband? Our God has intervened again and preserved you from harm. If you had gone instead of Irishum, such a defeat would have fallen on you and your family."

"Yes, I've thought of that."

Meira came into the garden to bring them some lemonade and overheard her mistress' words.

"May I say, Mistress, it saddened me, to learn how long my people suffered and starved in Samaria before they were delivered." But then her voice became excited. "Here is the wonderful thing. I've heard their deliverance came about because of four lepers. They discovered the Syrian army had fled, and the Lord led them back to Samaria with the good news. God moves in strange and wonderful ways. It is really true that His ways are not like ours."

Naaman smiled. "Strange and mysterious indeed." But a cold shiver ran down his spine as if his body remembered the terrible disease. "May the Lord bless those lepers."

After a moment, Adorina asked, "What will happen to Irishum?"

"He will be executed without doubt, as well as his commanders. I'm sad for all their families."

"A sad end indeed, and so dishonorable," his wife said.

That evening as they finished their supper and put the children to bed Naaman stretched out on a quilt. "I don't deserve the Lord's kindness."

"You are a good man," Adorina replied, "and your heart is where you believe the Lord wants it to be. Stop troubling yourself over this and go to sleep."

He kissed her, and as they had done since they were first married, fell asleep in each other's arms.

When Naaman entered the palace the next day, King Hadadezer grumbled, "I should have sent you to Samaria."

"What happens now?" Naaman asked.

"We must execute those responsible for this shameful defeat." The king saw the frown on Naaman's face and spoke quickly to reassure him. "Don't worry General, the royal guards will be in charge of the execution. Everyone knows how Irishum tried to kill you." He stopped before continuing to choose his words. "I must admit I made a mistake sending him to Tyre. He should have been executed when he tried to assassinate you. I never did tell you how I regretted that."

"You are King, Majesty," Naaman said. He was touched, however, by his friend's attempt to apologize. "A king does not need to explain his actions. I'm sorry the army will lose so many fine leaders along with Irishum."

Hadadezer decided to change the subject. "How is your family? I hear the chamberlain often comes to your home for supper."

Naaman shouldn't have been surprised that the king knew of old Mardokh's visits. Like all rulers, he had spies everywhere. "My Lady is well, my King. Ashur is in school as you know, and little Atalia is becoming more like her mother every day. Hadad our youngest, is the joy of our lives." The general had pleased the king by naming the little boy after him.

"Good. You have been blessed, old friend. When I think of what could have been your lot in life. . ." He didn't need to finish the sentence.

"Yes, Dezer, my God has blessed us and I am grateful you permitted me to go in search of Elisha."

Abruptly the king asked, "And what is the latest word from the prophet of Israel?"

"Why none, Majesty. I have not received any communication from the man of God since I left his house several years ago. You know that."

"Irishum became convinced you were receiving secret messages from the prophet on a regular basis. When I journeyed with the army near Samaria three months ago, that is all he could talk about."

At first, Naaman was surprised by the king's remarks. He then became offended. He realized the king wanted a response to his oblique accusation, but he took his time. Finally, he looked Hadadezer in the eye. "You are both mistaken, Majesty. You can ask any of my men or my family. Everyone will confirm that no word has ever been sent to me by Elisha the prophet."

The king knew his friend would deny the charge so he spoke of the task at hand. "You will join me to represent the army at Irishum's execution. My sentence will be carried out tomorrow morning and I want you to stand opposite me in the courtyard."

"At your command, Majesty."

"It will be a sad day for the families of the cowardly. I should have impaled his regiments as well." He stood and walked toward his veranda. "Until the morning," he said, nodding his head slightly to his friend."

Naaman came to attention and saluted before leaving the palace.

The next day began badly for Naaman's family. His son Ashur had a bad cough and had hardly slept that night. Little Hadad sounded like he had it as well. The king's physician, Lord Ninurta, arrived and examined the boys before Naaman had to leave for the execution.

"I'll be back as quickly as I can, my Love," he assured his wife when he saw her worried expression.

"We'll pray for your children, Master," Meira told him. "If the Lord is merciful, they'll be all right."

"May He hear your words, Meira," Naaman replied.

He drove his chariot to the palace, accompanied by his aides who rode on horseback alongside him. Upon reaching the palace courtyard, they found hundreds of on-lookers already gathered. Naaman knew his men would need a special resolve for what they would see and hear. Five heavy, pointed wooden stakes had been prepared for the impalement of Irishum's staff. A large wooden chopping block stood in place for the decapitation. As a high-ranking officer, the general would be beheaded, much to the displeasure of the crowd who always cried for lots of blood. Beheading would be too quick. Public executions were an exciting diversion from their ordinary lives.

The king arrived to much fanfare and applause. The queen would not attend, so other members of the court followed him and stood in the front row. Naaman and his men stood with the king's executioner on the opposite side of the yard. He gritted his teeth as the horrible impalements began and the crowd cheered louder and louder. The beheading of General Irishum would happen next. The spectators shouted obscenities and threw rotten fruit at the condemned nobleman.

Before placing his neck on the chopping block, Irishum turned toward Naaman and spit on the ground. "You should have died from your leprosy, Naaman. The gods could have eaten you away little by little, and I would have loved to hear you scream." Turning to the king he saluted with his fist and arm straight out. "I die in the service of my master the king as any warrior is proud to do." Kneeling down, he extended his neck to the executioner and when the crowd saw his head hit the ground they cheered at the top of their lungs.

Naaman had wanted the executions to take place at the army camp, in front of the men with whom they had served. The king's execution displeased all soldiers forced to be present.

A trumpet blast declared the end of the executions. The royal guards escorted the king and courtiers away from the courtyard. As Naaman went toward his chariot, the Captain of the Guard approached him.

"His Majesty commands your presence, General." Walking beside the guardsman they made their way up the stairs to the palace entrance.

"If you'll wait here a moment, General," the officer requested. "His Majesty is changing." Naaman nodded, glad to sit on one of the divans in the polished granite hallway. He had a bad taste in his mouth from what he had witnessed. He wished for some wine.

The king's steward came out and invited him in a few moments later. At that moment Naaman realized an important figure had been missing from the executions. Lord Mardokh, the Chamberlain, had not been there, and he became concerned.

Naaman was invited into the king's front room. "Some wine, Brother?" the king asked.

Naaman spoke in a subdued tone. "Yes, Majesty." He took a cup from the servant's tray.

"Thank the gods that's over," Hadadezer said.

Naaman knew his friend well enough to know that the king had enjoyed every minute of it. It was he who sent Irishum to lay siege on Samaria. "Yes, Majesty," was all Naaman could say.

"You seem preoccupied General," the king observed.

"My sons are ill, Majesty—some kind of cough. I'm concerned for them."

"I understand. I pray they will be well." He paused and looked a long while at his friend. "The reason I asked you here is to meet someone."

"Oh?" Naaman said.

The king walked to the door and said something to the guard outside. A few moments later a young man, perhaps in his early thirties, entered the king's apartment.

"General Naaman," the king began, "This is Hazael, a friend from my home region. He is to be Lord Mardokh's assistant. As you may have noticed, our venerated Chamberlain could not be with us due to a serious illness. Hazael will be filling in for him until he is restored to us."

"I am honored, Lord Hazael," Naaman said. He was once again at a loss for words. "You will be working with a man who has been like a father to us."

"It's true," Hadadezer said, "Let's drink to his health."

The men raised their cups with the king. "To Mardokh's health," they declared.

After some polite conversation, Naaman asked to be excused to see about his sons. The king nodded, preoccupied with Hazael. Naaman rejoined his friends who were waiting for him at the palace steps.

Naaman had a sinking feeling about his old friend. He feared he might not be allowed to see the old chamberlain again.

CHAPTER SIXTEEN

UNFORESEEN EVENTS

Two days later, Lord Mardokh, the respected prime minister of the King of Syria, breathed his last.

When the news of the death of their good friend reached Naaman's house, the family mourned his passing. The general rode to the palace immediately to ask for the honor of burying his mentor and friend. Given permission, the general's men removed the statesman's body from his home. One of the king's guards came by and insisted on speaking with Naaman.

"What is it?" the general asked.

Motioning Naaman aside, the young man said, "Forgive me, my Lord. My name is Esharra and I think you should know how your friend died."

Naaman, suddenly intent upon the guard's words, nodded. "Go on."

"I am betrothed to Naqiya, the chamberlain's personal housekeeper and assistant. She told me this morning that the old man received an unexpected visitor after retiring for the night. She didn't think anything of it until she heard the visitor leaving abruptly without saying goodnight. She thought it rude and unusual, but then went to her master's door. When he didn't respond, she assumed he had fallen asleep."

Naaman already guessed the rest of the story, and became angry.

"When she returned to her room, she sensed something wrong and went back to check on him," Esharra continued. "She found Lord Mardokh with a pillow over his face, already dead!"

"Did she recognize this late-night visitor?" Naaman asked.

"Yes, Mardokh's new assistant, Lord Hazael, my Lord."

Reining in his anger Naaman shook his head. "Where is your betrothed now, guardsman?"

"I'll bring her, my Lord." He hurried away and returned with the young woman a few moments later.

"This is Naqiya, General." The young lady bowed her head courteously.

Naaman smiled. "You have done the right thing in telling us about Hazael, young woman. But it puts you in great danger. We must take you to a safe place." Turning to Esharra he asked, "Is there somewhere you can hide her, perhaps with family or friends?"

"Yes," the guardsman said. "At my grandfather's farm downriver."

"Do you know where it is Naqiya?" Naaman asked the woman who nodded her head. "Good. I'll have two of my men take you there." He called Kapu and Ilani and instructed them to escort Naqiya immediately. "Take special care that you're not followed."

"I must go with her, General," the young man insisted.

"No," Naaman said. "You can't both be gone at the same time—it will only draw attention to yourselves. Say nothing and return to your post. If anyone asks where you've been, just say you've been comforting your betrothed over the death of her master."

The guardsman nodded and left the chamberlain's house.

Ishme and the remaining men chosen by the general, moved Mardokh's body to the temple of Rimmon and arranged for a funeral the next day. While there, a commotion outside announced Hadadezer's sudden arrival with his entourage.

"I'm sorry for the loss of your friend, brother," the king said.

He sounded sincere, but Naaman knew differently. "I appreciate being allowed to arrange his burial, Majesty," Naaman replied. He refused to acknowledge the king's words of condolence. Mardokh's murderer stood behind the king, and Naaman found himself helpless to do anything. Hazael nodded his head to the general politely, but Naaman looked away.

"It must be a state funeral, General," the king said. "He was well-loved by everyone at court."

"As you command, Majesty," Naaman said. "I will tell the priests to prepare for a larger funeral than I envisioned."

The king said, "Yes, by all means. I will honor my best and most trusted advisor. First Irishum and now Mardokh—who else am I to lose?"

A chill ran down Naaman's spine. Was it a veiled threat. Then he foolishly blurted out, "Only God knows, my King."

"Oh, you mean Elisha." The king said. His tone was tinged with sarcasm.

"Yes, he would know, Majesty," Naaman replied.

Hazael came closer, his movement like that of a mesmerizing snake. "The king's messengers tell us the prophet is traveling about the countryside. No one knows where he is."

Naaman became alarmed at this revelation. The prophet would be in danger if he were to enter Syrian territory.

"This prophet would be most welcome in Damascus," Hadadezer said. "Perhaps he could tell us if there will be a good harvest this year."

"He could tell you everything, my Lord," Naaman said. "Now with your permission, I will make arrangements for tomorrow."

The king said, "Yes, yes, of course. Carry on." He turned to Hazael, his new chamberlain, and spoke privately.

Naaman went to the temple of Rimmon, but his new faith did not allow him to enter. He spoke with the priests outside on the steps.

At the funeral the next day, Naaman and Lady Adorina remained on the steps, choosing to wait with some of Mardokh's friends who couldn't find a place inside. They listened with disdain to the tributes given by the king and the statesman's successor. After the service, when he shared with his wife what really happened, she wept the rest of the day.

"Only the king could have given the order for his death, Dorina," he whispered. "Hazael would not have been so bold as to murder Mardokh on his own."

Overall, Naaman had been pleased with the funeral. He appreciated everyone eulogizing how great a man the chamberlain had been. Except for the king, everyone's words were sincere and filled with true emotion. When they arrived home later that afternoon, there was someone waiting for them. Naaman was alarmed to see the king's guardsman at his house.

"Esharra," Naaman called to him. "Come in."

The young man followed the couple inside.

"Is Naqiya safe?"

"Yes, General, but there are men looking everywhere for her. They know she was Mardokh's housekeeper and may have seen the murderer. I don't know if she'll remain safe at the farm."

Naaman urged the young man to sit in the front room. "If that's true, then she is not far enough away. We'll move her tonight. Let's have some food, then we'll gather supplies and ride immediately to get my aides before dark."

The guardsman relaxed a little. "I'll eat in the kitchen with the staff. I'm not clean enough, General."

Naaman nodded and told Meira to see to Esharra's needs. A short time later, he and Naaman rode off toward the barracks to collect Ishme. They would ride together along the Abana River to the farm.

When they arrived, an overly cautious Kapu and Ilani didn't show themselves until they could see who had ridden in.

"What's wrong?" Ilani shouted. He and Naqiya walked out to meet them.

The three men dismounted and Naaman explained. "We need to get Naqiya away from here. There are soldiers looking for her. I only wish I knew where to take her."

"She could go to my sister's farm in Aleppo, my Lord," Kapu said. "She and my brother-in-law raise cattle and have very few neighbors or visitors."

"Excellent. What do you think Esharra?" Naaman asked. "She would be a much safer distance from Damascus."

The guardsman took the young woman's hand, and Naaman could tell by the expression on his face that he didn't like the idea of his love moving so far away. "Only if I can go with her, General. Can you release me from the Guards?"

"Well," Naaman began, "you could ask the Captain of the Guard for a leave of absence. But because everyone is looking for Naqiya, they'll know right away what we are doing. Just go with her, my friend. If your commander asks me I'll think of something. Naqiya tells me the old chamberlain was like a father to her."

"It's true General," Naqiya said. "That's what I called him."

"Kapu will go with you," Naaman told her. He is the finest archer in my regiment."

The young couple embraced briefly and Naqiya invited everyone inside.

The next morning, they prepared water skins and food for the journey. Kapu made sure his weapons were ready for any encounter, including extra arrows.

Before they left, Naaman prayed for the Lord God's protection over them, much to the young couple's surprise.

As Ishme and Ilani rode back to Damascus with him, Naaman shared his growing concern about the safety of the king. "I worry about him, brothers. With that serpent Hazael at his side, can we really trust the guards to protect him?"

"Captain Ruhubi is loyal to the king," Ishme said. "He will do all he can to protect him and the royal family. I'd bet my life on it."

"He's right, General," Ilani said.

Naaman nodded. "Very well, but I must get word to Hadadezer about being wary of the new chamberlain. He mustn't be alone with Hazael at any time."

"You must be the one to tell him, General," Ishme said. "He'll believe you."

They quickened their pace and reached Damascus before nightfall.

In the country of Israel, at the royal palace, King Joram sent for Elisha. Unfortunately, no one could find him. Instead, Shallum came in his place.

"I am the prophet's humble apprentice, my Lord King." Shallum couldn't control his voice, and he sounded like a young maiden. "Please tell me how the prophet may help you?"

Joram was angry Elisha hadn't come. "I need someone who really knows the man of God well. As his apprentice can you tell me about all of the miracles he has done?"

"No, but there is someone, Majesty," Shallum said. "Elisha's former servant Gehazi was with him for many years. He lives in the city and could tell you all about him, but he too is unable to come."

"By all that is holy," Joram shouted. "Why not?"

Shallum answered in an even more squeaky voice. "He's become a leper, Great King."

"A leper? Then what good is he to me?" The king's voice was growing louder. He paused for a moment. "Just a moment. If Elisha could heal Naaman, an enemy, couldn't he heal his own servant?"

Shallum knew better than try to answer the question.

Joram continued, thinking out loud. "Couldn't I keep this man at a distance, so he could answer my questions?"

"If you so desire, Majesty," Shallum answered. "I can ask him to come, but there will need to be a screen of some kind between you."

"Yes, yes, we can do all that. Bring him to me tomorrow," Joram ordered

Shallum bowed and the steward escorted him out of the king's presence.

The following day, Shallum went looking for Gehazi. He had a vague idea where the leper colony was located outside the city, but when he found the man's dwelling, the man refused to see him.

Shallum had to shout through a closed door. "But my Lord Gehazi, his majesty has asked for you by name. You must agree, or he'll send soldiers to bring you by force."

"What does he want?" the leper asked. "Did you explain things to him?"

"Of course, my Lord. The king is prepared to receive you."

"Very well, now go away! I'll go by myself in the morning."

Shallum left quickly. He had had enough of the filth and smell of the place.

The next day, Gehazi the leper, entered the palace by the back way. He wore his best robe and took care that his lesions didn't show. Four screens of woven palm fronds stood in the Audience Hall, surrounding his chair. He entered and sat behind the screens, waiting for the king.

When Joram entered, he asked, "Are you there, Gehazi?"

"Yes, Majesty. Do not be afraid. The Lord himself gave me this disease, and it cannot affect you."

"You mean your master, Elisha did this to you?"

"Yes and no, Great King," Gehazi answered. "I betrayed Elisha's trust and the Lord struck me down for my sin."

"I see, go on. Tell me about all the great things Elisha has done."

"Very well, Majesty," Gehazi replied. He then shared with the king everything he had seen and heard over the years with the man of God. "Through him the Lord parted the Jordan, my Lord—just like Joshua. Like Moses, he sweetened the bitter water for the sons of the prophets near Jericho so their land could be productive. Fresh water filled the valley from the mountains of Edom.

The Lord used Elisha in so many ways. I'm trying to remember them all," the leper mumbled.

"Go on—tell me more," Joram insisted.

"Well, there is the miracle of the pot of oil," Gehazi continued. He explained how Elisha multiplied the oil in one small pot so that a poor woman could have enough oil to pay her creditors and an over-abundance of it besides. He paused and thought some more. "He also prophesied that a barren woman and her husband would have a child, Majesty, and it happened. Little Jonah came along nine months later and I stood there at his naming ceremony. But then the boy died."

Surprised, the king could only say "Ah."

"Yes, it was very sad my Lord, but Elisha raised him from the dead and I saw everything. He did not use magic. The boy really died and Elisha breathed back into him the breath of life." After another moment, Gehazi went on. "And then we have the miracle of General Naaman, Great One."

"Ah yes, Naaman," Joram sighed. He felt annoyed for having been reminded.

Suddenly, the doors to the Audience Hall burst open and Amasa, the chamberlain, hurried in and bowed to the king. "Majesty, there is a widow here with her son who begs an audience. It's a dispute over some land, and the councilors said only you can decide the case. I'm sorry to interrupt, but she won't come back and is very persistent. You can perhaps settle this in a very short time."

Joram scowled. "Gehazi, remain where you are. I will hear this case."

Amasa returned with the woman and her son. They prostrated themselves before the king and he gave them permission to stand.

"I will hear your grievance, woman. Tell me what has happened." Joram sounded kinder than he intended,.

"My name is Elisheba, Majesty, I am a widow and this is my son Jonah. We have walked many leagues to reach you. It has been seven years since the great famine and the prophet Elisha told us to move away if we wanted to live. We moved to Joppa on the coast. I had no relative to leave on our land in Gath-helper and now it is occupied by another. I beg your mercy and ask you to give us our land back." She and her son bowed to the ground and awaited the king's pleasure.

Gehazi coughed several times, trying to get the king's attention. "Majesty," he whispered.

Annoyed, Joram walked back to the screen. "What is it?"

"Majesty, this is the woman I just told you about. She is the woman from Shunem whose son Elisha raised from the dead. My being here now has to be the Lord's doing, my king. He has brought me here for this moment."

"Is that you, Gehazi?" Elisheba cried out.

"Do not come near, my Lady," Gehazi warned. "I am now a leper."

"Is this true?" the king asked. "Are you the Shunemite woman whose son Elisha brought back to life?"

Elisheba fell on the floor in front of the king. "Yes, my King. It is true. The Lord has blessed us twice through his servant Elisha."

Joram now feared that this was indeed the Lord's doing. He called for Amasa. "Give this woman back everything that belonged to her. Arrange it. Include all the income from her land from the day she left Israel until now."

Amasa's eyebrows went up in surprise. "It will be done, Majesty."

Elisheba began to weep for joy and her son Jonah assisted her out of the Audience Hall.

The king sat down, amazed by what had just happened. Then, he said to the man behind the screen, "I agree with you, leper. This was no coincidence. The Lord has used us to help the woman and her boy. Elisha even works wonders when he is not here." Moving away from the screen he said, "You may go now, and I will see that you receive a reward for helping me this day."

"No, No," Gehazi exclaimed. "No reward, please, Majesty. My curse fell upon me because I took money for the Lord's work. I thank you for the gesture, but please, no reward."

"Very well, but accept our thanks," the king said. He left the Hall first, not wanting to look upon the person with whom he had been speaking. He ordered the palace servants to fetch water and lye and scrub down the Audience Hall for the rest of the day.

When Shallum returned home, Elisha met him at the door. "Where have you been?"

"Master, we did not know where you had gone. The king called for you and I went to tell him you were not here."

"What did he want?"

"He wanted to know about all your miracles. I only knew about a few, so I told him Gehazi would know so much more."

"Gehazi—that evil man. Well, he and the king deserve each other. The Lord is not pleased with either of them." He paused, then said more gently, "I want you to pack some things. We are leaving in the morning. The Lord is leading me north. I just don't know where yet."

Shallum smiled. "Yes, Master. I'll begin right away." He enjoyed traveling with his teacher, and began to wonder what excitement would come their way tomorrow.

CHAPTER SEVENTEEN

ACROSS THE BORDER

Shallum could sense that the Lord had been speaking to Elisha during the last few days. The elderly man mumbled to himself as if in a conversation.

"Listen to me, Shallum," Elisha said. "My mentor, Elijah, was afraid of Queen Jezebel and hid in a cave. She tried several times to kill him. My great master trembled with fear, but the Lord revealed to him the future of the kings of Israel and Syria. When I finally found where my master was hiding, the Lord spoke to me as well. He said, 'It is for you, Elisha, to go to Damascus, and accomplish what I commanded Elijah to do.'" He paused to drink a cup of water before continuing. "That night as I lay in the cave with my master, I couldn't sleep. I kept seeing images of what would happen to the people of Israel in the future."

The next day, Shallum saw how restless his master was becoming. He couldn't sit still and walked up and down the rows of vines. Finally, late in the afternoon Elisha decided they would start their journey in the morning.

When Shallum suggested taking a horse and wagon, Elisha said, "It is not appropriate for a servant of God to travel better than ordinary folk, young man. If God wanted us to travel faster, we would have been born with wheels instead of feet."

It didn't really matter to the apprentice. He enjoyed walking and meeting new and interesting people. On their first day, they encountered an elderly couple drawing water at a well.

"Where are you going?" Shallum asked. Curiosity was getting the better of him.

"To the Temple," the man replied.

Shallum smiled. "Ah, to Samaria then."

The woman became indignant. "No, to Jerusalem, young man. There is only one temple." She passed the wooden bucket to Shallum and the couple bid the two men farewell. The young apprentice shook his head, not understanding them at all.

Elisha said, "They're right of course. The Temple of Jerusalem is where the Lord meets with His people. It doesn't matter to the Lord that we've divided our kingdoms north and south. He chose Mount Zion forever."

"It's confusing, Master. We in the north believe the true temple is in Samaria, not Jerusalem."

The prophet removed a small pebble from one of his sandals. "I understand young one. When the Lord gave Solomon instructions for the construction of His House He said, 'I have heard your prayer and have chosen this place for myself as a temple for sacrifices.' So if the Lord chose Jerusalem, who are we to disagree?"

"If that's true, Master, then why don't we go there for Passover and the other feasts and festivals? I don't understand."

"In the beginning of the civil war between Israel and Judah, pilgrims from both kingdoms could still go up to Jerusalem. Now, we've drifted away from going, but the Lord is not pleased."

Shallum shook his head. "I beg forgiveness, Master. My mind can't concentrate. My stomach protests too loudly."

Elisha laughed. "Where is your discipline and self-control my son? It would do us all good to fast more. But I must agree with you. Let's see how good your skill with the bow is today. Go find our supper."

Shallum was pleased when he returned with two plump quail. The men cleaned and cooked them over the open fire, basting them with honey and goat's milk. After the delicious meal, they drank some wine and shared day-old bread purchased on the way.

Shallum sat rubbing his feet. "I'm glad tomorrow is the Sabbath, my feet need a rest."

"As do mine," Elisha said. "And remember, these feet are at least forty years older than yours."

A hundred miles away in Damascus, King Hadadezer awoke in the middle of the night with a severe pain in his stomach. His cries were so loud he awakened the whole palace.

Queen Atalila rushed to his side. "What is it dearest?"

The king pointed to the center of his abdomen. "It's as if someone were stabbing me here. Call Ninurta," he shouted, "and hurry."

When the healer arrived, he listened to the king's complaint and checked his majesty's right side first, relieved the appendix wasn't causing the discomfort. "There is some blood here, Majesty," the physician observed, indicating the king's sheets.

Surprised, Hadadezer shouted, "By the gods!"

Lord Ninurta went to the table where he had left his medicine bag and took out a jar of white powder, mixing some in a cup of wine.

"Drink this, Majesty. It's from the seed of the red poppy. It will soothe the pain for a time. I'll also give you a sedative to help you fall asleep again. I'll be here with you all night to make sure all is well. In the morning we'll see how you're doing." He gave the cup to the king who swallowed it in one gulp.

As the king began to drift off, he heard the queen ask the physician, "What's wrong with him, my Lord?"

"I cannot say yet, Majesty. It's not his appendix, but he's passing some blood. It means he's bleeding somewhere in his stomach or intestines. I'll know more in the morning, my Lady." The king heard her thank him, and Ninurta encouraged her to return to her own bed. "I'll stay here with the king."

The next day Hadadezer awoke without pain. His physician clapped for the steward and ordered a special morning meal for him. "Soft eggs, a little bread with no crust and some cow's milk."

"Is that all?" Hadadezer growled.

"For now, Majesty—we must see what is causing the attack. You may have a small perforation or hole in your stomach, and we must heal it so it will close up again. Eat only what I tell you."

"Such impertinence," Hadadezer exclaimed. That was all he said. He didn't want the excruciating pain to return. "Very well."

At that moment the new chamberlain pushed his way into the royal apartment. "I heard you are not well, Majesty. What's wrong?" Lord Hazael asked.

"The physician doesn't know. Cancel all my appointments for today. I will not see anyone."

"Very well, Majesty. I'll tell the ambassador from Tyre he must return home."

"He can go to the bottom of the sea for all I care. Leave us," Hadadezer shouted. He waved his hand and two guards came to escort the chamberlain out of the palace.

During the rest of the day the physician made additional tests, and prescribed meals that were gentle on the stomach. "We'll let you try solid foods in a few more days, my Lord King."

At day's end, the king exclaimed, "Well, Ninurta, what have all these tests shown?" The physician hesitated because he still didn't have an answer. "Well?" the king repeated more loudly.

"I am still unable to say, Great One. and I don't understand why you are still passing blood. With your permission, I'd like to stay another day."

"Out of the question," the king said. "You've upset my life enough. Leave us."

"Majesty." Ninurta bowed politely, and left.

One of the guards approached the physician. "My Lord, the queen calls you." He led the physician out onto her veranda.

The king overheard the guard, so he stepped onto his veranda and overheard his wife's conversation with the physician.

"Be truthful with me, Ninurta. What is causing it? the queen asked.

"I'm not sure, my Lady. I fear he may have several ulcers of the stomach. Keep spices from his food and give him no citrus. The pain will return if he aggravates the lining again."

"He won't die from it then?" she asked softly.

"No, my Queen. Not if he changes his diet and you can keep people like Hazael away from him. Anxiety and strong emotions will bring on these attacks again, and I can't be responsible."

The king frowned when he realized what the healer said. Physicians serve the monarch at the risk of their own life. Ninurta would die if the king died.

"Good then," Hadadezer growled. "You'd better figure it out healer."

On the dusty road heading north, Elisha and Shallum approached the border with Syria. The soldiers on duty let the two Israelites pass without difficulty. The prophet looked quite ordinary and the guards ignored him. The two Israelites had agreed to keep Elisha's name a secret from people they met on the road, or any officials.

That evening around their campfire, Shallum asked, "Do you know where the Lord is leading you, Master?"

Elisha nodded. "Yes my son, it is clear to me now. The Syrian king has fallen ill, and someone will come looking for me. We will wait for him in Damascus."

"Damascus?" Shallum gasped. "Why would you put yourself in such danger, Master?"

"Don't be alarmed," Elisha said. He chuckled as he rolled out his blanket for the night. "Nothing will happen to us. The Lord has told me He still has a lot of work for me to do."

"Oh, good," Shallum said. He began to breathe normally as he made his bed. "I hope He sees more years for me too. You realize you'll be arrested for coming here."

"Yes, but I also know the Syrians are afraid of our God. He has defeated their army twice now. Elisha lay down on the woolen cover. "And it was through my intervention that the Lord accomplished it. They will fear laying a hand on me."

"I believe you in my heart," his servant said. "It's in my head where I have trouble."

"The Lord is our rock and shield, Shallum. Of whom can we be afraid? Good words from King David."

"Thank you, my Lord," Shallum sighed, and fell asleep as soon as his head hit his blanket.

After travelling for two days, they reached the outskirts of the Syrian capital. This time, however, their reception by the guards at the city gates proved unfriendly.

"We don't want any more Israelites in our city," the soldier growled. He recognized their accent when they responded to a question, and made an issue of it.

"Peace, Soldier," Elisha said. calmly. "My God has sent me here and I mean you no harm."

"Sergeant," the soldier shouted. "Arrest these men."

An older man came toward them with reinforcements. "Come along," the guard said. He pushed the strangers ahead of him. They were forced to walk the short distance into the city until they reached the jail at the military garrison.

When their cell door was locked, Shallum, was frightened out of his wits. "Is it time to worry now, Master?"

In Damascus' royal palace, the king held his wife's hand. He saw by her face that she was worrying about him more than ever.

"You must eat some of this soup, my dearest," she said. "Have some bread."

The king shook his head, refusing to eat.

"The healer said you must eat to keep up your strength."

"It hurts when I eat, Atalia. I've told you time and time again. I've grown weary of the palace staff fussing over how much weight I am losing, and their attempts to smuggle me food." He pushed back his covers a bit. I wish old Murdoch was still alive. I am beginning to distrust Hazael. He's replacing my advisors by younger men who think as he thinks. Only Naaman remains from my old guard."

"I trust Naaman, Husband," Atalia said. "Is it wise to allow Hazael so much authority?"

"Women do not understand these things," Hadadezer replied. Seeing her face, he regretted the words as soon as they left his mouth.

For several months now, life for Naaman and his family had been peaceful and pleasant. Adorina had made the acquaintance of an Israelite couple who recently settled near the general's home. Naaman invited Levi and Rachel for a Sabbath meal.

Sitting together for the meal, Levi said, "It must have been the hand of the Lord that led us to each other. To find another family living in this pagan land who follow the Law of Moses is evidence of His guidance in all this."

Invited to light the Sabbath candles, Rachel recited the words Israelite women have prayed for hundreds of years. Naaman saw the smiles on the faces of the couple when they were introduced to Meira. They had lots of questions for her. Asking Adorina's permission, Rachel invited the servant to their home one day.

As the end of the evening, when the couple were leaving, Levi stood in the door way. "There is something you're missing in this house, brother. If you are truly a son of the covenant you must have a mezuzah on your door post. Where is it?"

Meira spoke up. "My master has made so many changes in his life, my Lord. I haven't told him about that yet."

"That's no problem, my dear," Rachel said. "You simply write the *Shema* on a small piece of parchment and place it on the doorpost. Usually we touch the mezuzah and bring our fingers to our lips when we enter and leave our homes."

"The *Shema?*" Naaman repeated.

"Yes, brother," Levi said. 'Hear O Israel the Lord is our God, the Lord is One.' The family recites it at the front door in the morning and evening. It is a way to instill in our children our central belief that there is only one God."

Naaman smiled. "There is so much to remember. How good of the Lord to bring you into our home to teach us."

"And for us to meet and know a Syrian now son of Abraham, my Lord General," Levi said.

Naaman put his hand on Levi's shoulder. "Well, there will be a mezuzah on my door the next time you come to visit."

They bid their guests good night, and went back into the house. No sooner had they returned to the front room than they heard hoof beats approaching the house. Naaman walked to the door to see who could be arriving so late in the evening.

"Ishme," Naaman said. "This is a surprise."

"Sorry General," his friend said. "This is important, and I think you'll be pleased."

"Good. Pleasant news is always welcome." Adorina walked back to the foyer to see who it was and smiled at the captain.

The three of them seated themselves in the front room. Ishme said, "I've the most astonishing news, my friends. I've seen Elisha. He's here in Damascus."

His friends were shocked. "Elisha? Here in Damascus?" Naaman said. "Are you sure?"

"Oh yes," the captain told him. "He and his servant are in jail."

"What?" Naaman groaned. He jumped up from his chair. "We must get him out of there. What happened?"

"When I passed the barracks this evening, I met an old friend and we talked for a while. He said there were at least twenty Israelites arrested at the city gates this week and we walked back to where they're locked up. I looked twice to be sure, but I recognized the prophet immediately. I don't think he saw me, though."

Naaman stood and paced back and forth. He stopped and asked, "How do I get him out of there without drawing attention to who he is?"

Ishme thought a moment. "Send Kapu with me to the jail carrying an order from you to interrogate the two prisoners. You can say you are hoping to get information about any Israelite soldiers who might be hiding in the hills around the city."

"Yes, that could work," Naaman said. "No one would dare refuse an order from the king's general. You can use one of the small military wagons to bring the prophet to my house."

"Very good, General."

"Call for Meira, dearest," Naaman said.

His wife went to call her When she came, Naaman told her about Elisha. She became excited at the news.

"May the Lord be praised," Meira sighed.

Naaman said. "This is another miracle. Now you must help me put the words of the Lord on my doorpost right now. I want to show the man of God that we are observant children of Abraham."

She nodded, and the two women left to gather their writings materials.

"Elisha will recognize you Ishme," Naaman said. He walked with the captain out to his horse. "Once you have him in the wagon, act as if this is all normal procedure. Don't tell him you're bringing him to my house. Just say he is going to be questioned by one of your superiors. Let's surprise him."

Ishme nodded and then began to chuckle. "But General, Elisha is a Seer. How can any of this be a surprise?"

CHAPTER EIGHTEEN

HAZAEL

Elisha was watching through the bars of the cell when a soldier came and spoke to the guards on duty. He showed them a message and they nodded and led him toward the prisoners.

"They're in number seven," one of the guards said. The soldier, who had been given the key by the guards, stopped in front of their cell and unlocked the door.

"Follow me," the soldier ordered the elderly man. "You too, young man. Come along."

Elisha stood and walked to the door behind Shallum. He felt like he recognized the soldier, but walked behind him as they went outside and got into a small wagon.

"Sit beside the driver," the soldier ordered.

The driver nodded to them. Mounting his horse, the officer led the way toward the western city gate. They passed through it and moved down the road in the direction of several villas. Pulling up in front of one, the soldier dismounted and waited for Shallum to help his master down.

Elisha looked at the beautiful house then followed the soldier to the front door. He saw the mezuzah immediately and was surprised that a Jewish family could be living in Damascus. He touched it with his fingers and lifted them to his lips. The soldier encouraged him to open the door and enter the foyer.

"Peace be with you, my Lord Elisha—in the Name of the Lord God of Israel," Naaman said. His voice trembled with emotion. He knelt on one knee before the man of God and bowed his head.

"Lord Naaman, bless my soul. May the Lord be praised indeed." He walked over and helped raise Naaman to his feet, and embraced him in a fatherly way. They laughed happily, patting each other on the back. When Adorina and the children came forward Elisha also embraced them. "May God's blessing rest upon all who live in this house," he said. "What a happy reunion the Lord has given me."

"Come and be seated my friends," Naaman said. He led his guest into the front room. "My wife will prepare some refreshments while we talk." He turned and called Meira to come forward. "This is Meira, my Lord. She is the reason for my miracle. It is her faith in the Lord and you, that brought me to Samaria."

Meira, more than Naaman, had trouble controlling her emotions as she approached the prophet. "It is my master's faith, too, my Lord Elisha, that made it happen," she insisted. "I am only an instrument of the Lord."

In a kind voice Elisha said, "Well spoken." He stood and placed his hand on her head and prayed a special benediction on her. It moved her to tears and when he finished, he wiped them away with his fingers. "Our Lord will bless you my dear. As long as Naaman's name will be remembered, so will yours. You have been faithful by remaining here to bring our friends into the Light. That is a benediction in itself."

When Elisha sat down, a young voice behind him asked, "Are you really a prophet?"

"Who wants to know?" the elderly man teased.

"This is my son Ashur, my Lord," Naaman said.

"Well, I am a prophet my boy. When we have a moment, I'll tell you about it."

Naaman sat back in his chair. "I too have many questions, my Lord."

"Good," Elisha said. "Our Lord will have all the answers."

When all Naaman's questions about the faith had been answered, he took the prophet out into his garden to show him a special place. He stood in front of two small mounds of earth covered by grass.

"Do you remember the two bushels of soil I took from your garden?"

"Yes. I didn't understand your request at first, until the Lord revealed to me why you needed them."

"It is here upon this earth I pray every day," Naaman explained. "I know there is no power in the dirt, but it helps me remember the land of my deliverance. In a sense, I felt it drew me closer to you."

"And here I am, my son," Elisha said. "While this may not be a sacred or holy spot, it is a place for remembering."

The King of Syria was sitting up when the captain of the guard entered the king's bedchamber.

Captain Ruhubi said in a quiet voice, "Apologies, Majesty."

King Hadadezer didn't turn or try to look at him. "What is it?" he mumbled.

"I learned something from one of the guards at the jail, Majesty. It concerns two Israelite prisoners held there overnight. One is an elderly man, the other much younger—possibly his son or a servant." The king wasn't paying much attention to the man's report.

"The guard heard the younger man address the elder as 'master' and he said the older man carried himself with authority like an official. The next morning, General Naaman's men came for the same two men and took them to his home."

Hadadezer perked up. "Naaman's men you say?"

The captain nodded.

"One is older and has a servant, hmm. Why were they thrown in jail?" the king asked.

"We've had too many foreigners coming to the capital, your Majesty. Many are thrown into jail to discourage them from staying here. The guard told me that when he asked the old man why he came to Damascus, the Israelite said his god told him to come."

"It's Elisha," the king shouted. He became suddenly excited. "Oh, by the gods. Is it possible? It has to be him. Yes, yes." He got out of bed much to the alarm of the captain of the guard. "Bring Hazael to me at once," he ordered.

Then, he clapped his hands and the royal steward rushed in. "My robe." the king shouted. "And I want to wash myself, hurry." While he cleaned up, the Chamberlain entered his room.

"Hazael," the king said, grabbing a towel to dry his face. "I'm sending you on an important mission. Go to Naaman's villa and ask him the name of his guest. Don't leave until you've learned who it is—is that clear?"

"Of course, Majesty."

The king waved his hand as if to get rid of the interruption.

"And now, Captain," Hadadezer said turning back to the officer of the guard. "If it is Elisha the prophet, we must provide a place for him to stay. What about Lord Athan's villa? He's in Sidon for a few months. Could we put the holy man there?"

Captain Ruhubi thought for a moment. "Of course Majesty. Their servants are presently keeping the house ready."

A suddenly energized king responded. "Excellent. Go and tell them they are to prepare for my guest."

Ruhubi saluted, turned, and left.

The queen entered the room. "You shouldn't be up, Husband," she scolded. "What are you doing? Let me help you get back into bed."

Hadadezer would have none of it. "We believe the man of the god of Israel is in Damascus, my Love. Remember? He's the man who healed Naaman." He saw the look in her eyes and said, "Yes, I want to know if he can heal me."

Atalia let out a long breath. "Praise Rimmon, Husband. Be kind to this prophet, Dear One. You know how your temper flares up."

"Don't presume to order me about, Madam," he replied. The king smiled, because he knew his wife could see he was feeling better.

Darius, Naaman's steward, interrupted the mid-day meal to announce a visitor had arrived at the villa. Naaman entered the foyer, surprised by who awaited him. "The king's Right Hand—Lord Hazael, what an unexpected pleasure."

"Apologies, Lord General, but I'm here on the king's business."

"Oh?" Naaman said. "Well in that case, would you care to join us at our meal, my Lord?"

"You are kind, General, but this will only take a moment. His majesty wants to know the name of the guest who has been here the past two days?"

Naaman frowned, disappointed that the identity of the prophet had been discovered. "Elisha the Seer is staying with us, Lord Chamberlain. I did not bring him to his majesty because of the king's state of health."

Hazael shook his head. "You didn't bring him, General, because you and your men broke him out of the king's jail." He waved his hand. "But nothing more will be said about it. After all, his majesty will certainly ask the prophet to heal his sickness." He nodded to Naaman, and said, "Please forgive the intrusion." Hazael saluted, then went back to his chariot.

Naaman stood at the door and watched the man ride off with his guards.

When he returned to his friends at the dining table, he said, "I've bad news I'm afraid."

"I have been found out," Elisha said.

"Yes, my Lord. The king sent his chamberlain to learn your identity."

"Hazael, you mean," Elisha said. "The Lord God knows who he is, as do I. You must allow me to speak with him when he returns."

"Of course, my Lord. Do you already know he's coming back?"

"Yes, he'll come to ask a question from the king, and will move me to another location." He saw the concern on his host's face. "Do not worry, my friend Naaman. I have a few more years to live."

Naaman smiled. "It must be a blessing to know what is going to happen before it does." Then something suddenly struck him. "Wait a moment, Lord Elisha. That means you knew all along that I would be healed, didn't you?"

Elisha smiled, smoothing his beard with his fingers. "The Lord allowed me to see you coming up from the river the seventh time, my boy. But if you hadn't obeyed me, I would have seen a very different future for you. To see what will happen can be a blessing or a curse."

Shyly, Lady Adorina spoke up, "And what about our family's future, Lord Prophet? Can you see that far?"

"Normally my Lady, I don't reveal those kinds of things to people who are friends. In the end, they don't really want to know. But I know that Ashur will grow up to be a good man and have a family of his own—as will his brother. The beautiful Atalia will wed a righteous man and have four daughters." He paused and closed his eyes. "I also see a silver crown of hair upon your head, my Lady, but your beauty will not fade with age." Pointing to Naaman his voice grew deeper, "he will serve the Lord all his days, and like Moses, old age will not leave a mark on him."

Naaman and his wife stood and embraced each other. Adorina wiped tears from her face. Naaman said, "My boys already think I'm too old, my Lord, so they won't be glad to hear that." He stood and led his guess into the front room.

"You said during the meal you might take me down to the river, General," Elisha said. "Is that still a possibility?"

"Yes, we can go now if you choose." Naaman said. The man of God agreed, and Naaman told his wife they would return in a short while.

Later, when they returned home, a wagon and four guardsmen were waiting for them.

"Captain Ruhubi sends his greeting, my Lord General," one of the guards declared. "The king has arranged for your guests to be moved to a villa he is providing nearby. We are here to help them move."

"I see," Naaman said. It was all he could do to keep the exasperation out of his voice. "And you are going to do that now, young man?"

"As the king commands, General."

"Very well, wait here," Naaman ordered. He led Elisha into the house. Once inside he said, "I can't let you go with them, Master. I can't protect you while you are in their hands."

Elisha put a hand on Naaman's shoulder and the general felt a surge of energy course through his body. "Be at peace, my boy," he said. "Your king only means well for me and is trying to be kind. We'll go with them. Remember what I told you—the Lord has a lot more for me to do before I die."

"As the Lord wills," Naaman said.

"When we are settled, wherever it is we're going, you must come each day so we may continue our lessons in the Torah," Elisha said.

"With pleasure, teacher. I will be there."

"Good." Elisha turned to Shallum. "Get our things, my friend. We mustn't keep the king's men waiting." The way the young man looked at Naaman, he could tell he didn't want to leave the safety of Naaman's house. Shallum nodded and went to pack what few things they had. When he finished, and they were in the wagon, Naaman and his wife stood at the front door and watched them being carried away.

Naaman put his arm around Adorina's waist. They found it difficult to speak. Finally Adorina said, "The Lord will be with them."

Early in the afternoon of the next day, Elisha sat on the front porch of the large house the king had provided them. He and his apprentice couldn't believe their luxurious surroundings. Suddenly he heard the familiar noise of camels grunting as they made their way toward the house.

"Shallum," he called.

His apprentice hurried to his master's side. The young man's eyes grew wide as he watched the tall graceful animals approaching. Each camel carried not only a rider but a load of what appeared to be supplies of food and gifts wrapped in colored cloth.

Captain Ruhubi rode up on horseback and dismounted. Suddenly a chariot raced up the road in a great cloud of dust and stopped in front of the villa.

"Hazael," Elisha whispered, knowing he was about to face the inevitable.

"These supplies and gifts are but a sampling of the finest wares of our city. They are gifts to you from the king," the young chamberlain said.

"We are touched by the king's generosity," Elisha said. "Please come and rest yourself while the men unload the animals. It will give us time to talk." This pleased Hazael and he bowed his head, following the prophet inside.

The servant poured them each a cup of wine. "Leave us, Shallum," Elisha ordered. His apprentice nodded and left.

Sipping the cool sweet beverage, Hazael then put his cup on the table. "Your servant, Hadadezer, King of Syria, has sent me to ask, 'Will I recover from this illness?'"

Elisha stared at his cup before answering. "Go and say to him, 'You will certainly recover.'" The prophet paused for a moment, then stood. "But the Lord has revealed to me, Hazael, how he will in fact die." The words caused Hazael to stand as well. Elisha looked him closely until Hazael was forced to look away. Elisha knew that Hazael was aware of what was to come and he couldn't face the man of God. Suddenly Elisha sat down again and began to weep.

"What is wrong, my Lord?" Hazael asked, disturbed by the sight.

It took Elisha some time to regain control of himself. Finally he stood again and walked toward one of the windows. "I weep because I can already see the harm you will do to my people. You will set fire to our fortresses and kill our young men with the sword. You'll dash our children to the ground and will kill many women about to give birth."

Hazael was shocked not only by the man's words, but that the prophet was able to see into his future. He asked, "How can I do such things? I am as low as a dog. How can I accomplish them?"

Elisha sighed, deciding to tell Hazael everything the Lord had revealed long ago to his teacher, Elijah, who passed it on to him. "The Lord has shown me that you, Hazael, will become the next king of Syria."

Hazael shouldn't have been surprised by the old man's words—first about the king's health, and then about his succession to the throne. Elisha saw by the trace of a smile on Hazel's face that his words had pleased him.

"May your god be praised for such kind words, my Lord, first for my king, and then for me, his servant."

Elisha nodded and stood to escort the chamberlain to the door. The goods brought by the caravan had been unloaded and stored in various rooms of the villa. Captain Ruhubi saluted and followed Hazael's chariot as they led the long train of camels back to the city.

At dusk, Naaman and his family arrived at Elisha's temporary dwelling for a wonderful supper prepared by Shallum and the household servants. Elisha showed them all of the merchandise the king sent as gifts. "Forty camels were needed to deliver it all," Shallum explained as they passed from room to room filled with the king's generosity.

After the meal, while Shallum played with the children on the front porch, Elisha told his friends about Hazael's question from the king and the Lord's answers about the future.

Naaman became immediately alarmed. "You must leave here at once, my Lord," he declared. "The king's life and yours too are now in jeopardy, my friend." Elisha looked puzzled, but the general added, "By telling Hazael the future, he will make sure your prophecy comes true. If he chooses to kill you, then there would be no one to prophecy who would replace *him*."

Elisha said, "No, no. I told you, my friend, it is the Lord's will I stay on this earth a while longer."

"Yes, I know my Lord, but for Israel's sake we must get you to safety. Ishme and my aides will take you to the border on the back roads that only my men know. Please, my teacher, do this for me."

Elisha wrinkled his brow and thought about Naaman's warning. "All right, my son. We will place our lives in your hands. This may also be the Lord's will."

"Let Him be praised," Naaman whispered. "I'll take my family home, then we'll be back for you. Pack only what you deem necessary for the journey."

Elisha nodded and went with Shallum to pack their baggage.

A short time later, Elisha and Shallum climbed into the wagon, and with Naaman and his men on horseback riding on each side, they rode quickly out of town. With the moonlight to guide them, they followed what were only shepherd's trails.

"We should reach the border by morning," Naaman assured Elisha.

"He can't hear you, General," Shallum said. "He's sound asleep."

CHAPTER NINETEEN

FLIGHT

King Hadadezer of Syria had grown impatient by the time his new chamberlain entered the royal apartment. "Where is he?" the king shouted. His face had turned the color of an overripe pomegranate. "You should have returned with him long ago."

"Calm yourself, Majesty," Hazael said. "Remember your stomach."

"What did Elisha say?" the king shouted.

"He told me that you would certainly recover, Majesty."

"Is that all?"

"Yes, Great One. I thought the good news would please you."

The king took a moment to calm down. "It is good indeed," he said. "If Elisha says it will happen—it will happen. Bring him to me tomorrow so we may show him our appreciation."

"Yes, my Lord." Hazael bowed and left the room.

That evening, the royal couple was more relaxed than they had been in a very long while and were intimate for the first time since the king became ill. Afterwards, the queen fell asleep in his arms and he gently slipped out of bed and returned to his bedchamber.

In the middle of the night, Hazael entered the king's chamber unnoticed. No one heard the king cry out as his chamberlain pushed a wet towel down hard onto the king's face. With his mouth covered, Hadadezer struggled with all his might but Hazael pressed down harder. The king's face turned red, then purple until he gasped his last. Holding the cloth, Hazael wrung it out into a vase of flowers and placed it with the other used towels beside a ceramic basin.

He turned the king's body and arranged the bed linens to look as if the king were still asleep when he died. Then, as silent as death, he slipped out of the chamber.

Hazael grinned, because in the morning, the palace would learn that Elisha's prophecy had come true, and that he had become the new king of Syria.

Out in the Syrian countryside, Naaman and his six travelers were barely visible in the moonlight. He could see, however, that everyone was weary. They had gone about a league from Damascus. He stopped at a small stream so they could rest.

"You must go back, General," Ishme said, bringing Naaman a cup of water. "When the king discovers Elisha is gone and you along with him, he'll not be pleased and will most certainly arrest your family."

"I've been thinking the exact same thing ever since we left," Naaman said.

"I agree my son," Elisha said. "You must go home to protect your loved ones."

"Very well, but Captain Ishme is in charge of getting you safely to Israel."

"You can count on us, General," Ishme said.

"The Lord be with you," Naaman said. He turned his horse around and urged the animal into a gallop. His heart pounded to the rhythm of the hoof beats, and he was so anxious, he didn't stop for anything. The moon had slipped below the horizon when he reached home. His steward heard him arrive, and rushed out to cool down the horse and put it in the stable. Naaman tried to slip quietly into his bedchamber, but Adorina heard him. He encouraged her to go back to sleep.

"Everything's all right," he whispered, and she soon drifted off again. Naaman couldn't sleep and whispered a prayer, thanking the Lord he had made it home. He listened to her breathe and moved closer so he could feel her heart beat. His mind continued to race, but eventually fatigue overcame him.

Naaman hadn't slept long before someone disturbed his rest.

"Master, wake up," his steward said.

The general sat up, rubbed his eyes and got out of bed. Wrapping a sheet around himself, he followed his servant into the hallway.

"Captain Ruhubi is in the front room, my Lord," his steward said. "Something's happened." Naaman nodded and hurried into the room.

"What is it Captain? Is it about Elisha?"

"No, my Lord. King Hadadezer is dead. The servants found him in bed this morning. I've come because I know you were his friend."

Shocked by the news, Naaman had to sit down. "Dezer. . ." he mumbled. Even though the king had treated him badly, he still remembered with affection his childhood friend and the adventures they had growing up. "Thank you Captain, it was kind of you to come."

"Hazael has proclaimed himself king," Ruhubi added. "Already there are many changes at the palace. Everyone loyal to Hadadezer has been dismissed, including me. The queen has been sent back to her family up north, and guardsmen escorted her out of the city this morning."

"That can't be," Naaman exclaimed. "It's against our tradition. Atalia must bury her husband in the manner of our people. Hazael cannot do this." His emotions nearly overpowered him. The sadness of losing his friend, and now the anger toward Hazael needed a release. He ordered the steward to bring him his horse, and then he rushed back into his chamber for his clothes.

"Let's ride," Naaman said, and Captain Ruhubi joined him. They urged their steeds into a gallop, racing up the road into the hills. When the horses began to grow weary, Naaman found a rocky place near some terebinth trees. Tethering the horses in a grassy area, the two men moved toward a cluster of boulders. Naaman put one foot up on a large rock and placed his elbow on his knee. Resting his chin on his fist, he could see Damascus in the distance, nestled in a veil of mist.

"This is precisely what Elisha told me would happen. The Lord revealed all this to him and he told me. I just didn't realize my old friend would die so soon."

"That is not all, General" Ruhubi said. He leaned against the side of a large boulder. "You're not going to believe this. Old Ninurta, the good physician, told me before he ended his own life, that the king did not die a natural death in his sleep. He was smothered to death. He found linen threads in his mouth."

"That jackal's spawn," Naaman shouted. "So, Hazael begins his reign with murder and treachery. This is a tragic day indeed." Suddenly, his eyes showed fear, and he stood up straight. "Adorina and my babies," he whispered. Leaping onto his horse he raced back toward town with Ruhubi trying to keep up.

When they reached home, Naaman found Adorina already in the dining room, but the children were still asleep. He told her about the king's death, and she collapsed in tears. "Poor Atalia," she whispered.

The children came out to see what was happening, and Meira was with them. Naaman told her to take the children away until he could speak with them. She nodded and led little Atalia and the boys back to their bedchambers.

"I must go to the palace at once," Naaman said. "Hazael will expect me to come as soon as I learn of the king's death."

"I can't come with you, General, but I would like to join your regiment—if you'd have me, that is," Ruhubi said.

"Wait for me here, young man. Protect my family. If Hazael lets me live, then I would be honored to have you join us." Not knowing if he would be able to return to his wife and children, he clenched his fists and tried to control his emotions. Rushing outside, he jumped back onto his horse and rode to the palace.

Naaman made his way into the royal apartments with a heavy heart. He could tell by those he met in the hallways that a major turnover in staff and personnel had already occurred. A man who Naaman thought must have replaced Hazael as chamberlain, asked him to wait outside the Hall of Audiences to be announced.

"General Naaman is here to see you, Majesty," the man declared. He indicated the general standing in the hallway.

Naaman looked into the hall and could see Hazael seated on the throne. He was receiving the ambassadors and delegates from Syria's neighbors living in the city. Naaman knew they had come to express their condolences and offer support for Hadadezer's successor. Naaman couldn't just stand there doing nothing, so he walked back and forth in the hallway.

"Make him wait a bit, Irhuleni," he heard the king reply. "Bring in Lord Ba'asa first." The new chamberlain nodded and left to carry out his sovereign's command. Naaman frowned at the new king's discourtesy.

When allowed to enter, Naaman saw a stranger standing at the king's side.

"We welcome our beloved General," Hazael said.

Naaman went down on one knee and saluted the king.

"Stand, my Lord. Let us speak as friends." Turning to the man at his right, he said, "This is my cousin Ba'asa. He will now replace you as General of the Army and will be my Right Hand."

Naaman saluted his replacement, who returned the gesture.

"General Naaman, I have decided to allow you to enter into well-deserved retirement. Buy a farm or move to the coast where they tell me life is easier." He motioned to Ba'asa, who walked down the steps and handed a leather pouch to his predecessor. The king said, "Here is the sum allowed for your pension. You will receive it at each new moon, along with the thanks of your people." He waited for Naaman to respond and smiled like a cat with its paw on the mouse's tail.

Naaman cleared his throat, trying to find the words for a response. "First of all Majesty, I am deeply saddened by the death of my friend. I will be the first to admit I am uncertain as to what kind of life I would have as a farmer or fisherman." He paused and saw the amusement on the king's face. "I am grateful for your permission to leave the army and wish every success and blessing to Lord Ba'asa."

"Then it's done," Hazael exclaimed. "Well said."

Realizing the king meant his audience had concluded, Naaman turned to go.

Hazael, however, hadn't finished. "Will you ask Elisha to come at his convenience, my Lord?"

"Elisha has already returned to his home in Israel, Majesty," Naaman answered. He had trouble, however, keeping a straight face.

"Gone you say? And all the goods we gave him?" Hazael said. "I am not pleased with this revelation."

"The gifts are all there in the villa according to the servants, Majesty," Naaman replied.

The king waved his hand in dismissal.

As Naaman left the hall, he could hear the angry words of the new king. "Find the prophet and bring him back." Naaman grinned. He knew the king's Right Hand would be unsuccessful. By now, Elisha would be safely home in Samaria.

Naaman rode directly to the house of his friends Levi and Rachel and shared the news with them.

"Where will you go my friend?" Levi asked.

"I don't know. I hoped you might have some ideas. I would like to move closer to the land of your people and visit the Temple one day. Perhaps I could buy a farm."

Rachel, normally quiet, spoke up. "What about my family in Yokneam, Husband? It overlooks the Jezreel Valley and the land is rich and fertile. Mount Carmel is nearby, and there are good farms all around."

Her husband began pulling on his dark beard. "Yokneam," her husband repeated. Looking at his wife, he saw her gentle nod. "All right," he said, "but Rachel and I are coming with you. If Hazael is as opposed to Israelites as you say, my friend, none of us is safe."

"I haven't spoken to Adorina yet, but I know in my heart we must leave tonight. Can you be ready? It might mean life or death if Hazael changes his mind about letting me go." He paused to collect his thoughts. "We'll need two wagons and horses but your neighbors cannot know you're coming with me. That alone will put you in danger."

Naaman rode home and told Adorina what had happened. She was so overcome, she fell into his arms. "Leave our home, Beloved? It will be like cutting out my heart to leave this place." She wept bitterly, devastated by it all. "I am saddest for you, my Beloved," she continued, weeping on his chest. "Naaman, my general—no longer a commander of men."

"Yes," her husband sighed, moved by her words. "But am I still commander of your heart, my Love?" That made her sob again, and he let her cry until there were no more tears. "I will tell the children, my dearest," Naaman said, "but first I must deal with the young man waiting for me." She nodded and lay down across their bed, trying to dry her eyes.

Walking toward the guardsman, Naaman said, "Captain Ruhubi. I have a proposition for you. Hear me out before you respond." The young man nodded and Naaman continued. "You can join the army if you wish, but King Hazael will always be suspicious of your loyalty—that's why he's let you go. On the other hand, I need a guard for my family in the days ahead. I would like you to come with us. We are hoping to buy a farm further south, but it could be a dangerous journey." He waited for the ex-officer to fully understand his proposal. "I know my aides will want to stay here in the army, so I will need a man I can trust. You are good with sword and bow or you wouldn't be a guardsman. Are you married?"

"I'm a widower, my Lord."

"I'm sorry for your loss, my friend. Perhaps in the new life ahead of us, you might find a wife." He thought of something else and said, "You do know we are followers of the God of Israel. Our lives will be different than what you're used to."

"I know my Lord. Everyone at the palace knows of your miracle."

"Good. Do you need more time to make up your mind?"

"I'm ready to go with you. All I have is a small sack and the horse I brought with me. Not much for five years of service is it?"

Naaman shook his head. "Not much at all. There is also an Israelite couple making the journey with us. We are leaving tonight. Since you can't stay at the barracks, do you need a place to stay?"

"Yes, I'm afraid so."

"Well, if you don't mind staying in our servant's quarters, you are welcome here and can take your supper with us." The man nodded and thanked him.

Later that afternoon, Naaman's three aides returned from accompanying Elisha to the Israelite border. They came to Naaman with their report.

"We left Elisha at the Jordan crossing we used before, General," Ishme told him. "He should be in Samaria by now, but he told us he also has other places to go."

Naaman smiled. "That sounds like him."

That evening, Naaman and his wife found it difficult to bid farewell to Darius their steward and the other servants. As part of their family now, Meira would come with them.

Captain Ishme had the most difficult time in saying goodbye. He didn't want to see Naaman leave. "Don't be surprised if we show up some day on your doorstep," he said. Then he embraced everyone in the family.

"That goes for us too," Kapu said speaking for himself and Ilani.

After sunset, the small party left Damascus and followed one of the back roads Ishme had taken with Elisha the day before. A half-moon provided enough light to see the way. Naaman rode out front, with Ruhubi bringing up the rear.

When they neared a small stream in the middle of the night, they stopped to rest. Adorina watched Meira lifting her hands to heaven. "What are you doing Meira?"

"I am praising the Lord with the words of David, my Lady. 'You are a shield around me, O Lord. You bestow glory on me and lift up my head.'"

"How do you know the words? They're not in the books of Moses are they?"

"No, but I remember my mother singing them to me whenever we traveled as children. We didn't go far, not even a league away, but she found them comforting. I haven't thought of them for many years."

"Recite them again, Meira. The children can learn them too," her mistress suggested. The travelers listened to the children repeating the words as they continued down the bumpy old road.

As dawn approached, Naaman slowed the pace so he could ride alongside Levi and Rachel's wagon. "Did you have trouble selling your store and house, my friends?"

"No, not at all," Levi answered. "I knew my Syrian competitor would be delighted to see the back of me and he bought them both. He thinks were moving to Tyre." They rode awhile in silence until Levi asked, "Are you sure this road is safe, General?"

"Ishme assured me that there are fewer bandits here than on the main road. But I'm not worried about them, my friend. It's the new king's guards that concern me most." Even though the travelers had to stop frequently to rest the horses, they traveled a good distance that day and encountered no one else on the road.

In the evening as they sat together around the fire, the two boys shared what they had seen on this, their great adventure. When Ruhubi managed to bring down several partridges with his archer's skills for supper, the boys wouldn't leave him alone. They begged him to let them shoot an arrow. Young Ashur, now eleven, and his brother eight, also enjoyed teasing their ten-year old sister. In the end, though, Atalia always got the better of them. She also proved a great help to Meira and her mother.

After they had eaten, Naaman said, "Brother Levi, will you read something from the scroll of Moses?" He handed it to his friend, who took it, kissed it first, and then, opened the scroll to a portion from the Book of Moses called "Names" or "the going out."

"See, I am sending an angel ahead of you," he read, "to guard you along the way and to bring you to the place I have prepared." Levi rolled up the scroll, kissed it again, and said, "Since we are on a journey as well, I take comfort from these words, my friends. I believe the Lord is sending an angel ahead of us even now, to guard us along the way. He will bring us to a place we don't even know about yet, but the Lord knows. He is preparing it for us all."

No one spoke for a few moments, then Adorina said, "You have chosen the right words, Levi. It is comforting to know the Lord is with us. I'm not sure about angels though. Are all of them friendly?"

Rachel smiled. "They are the Lord's messengers, Adorina. That's the meaning of their name. Fortunately, in the writings of Moses, angels are always good."

"With those encouraging words," Naaman said, "we should turn in. I'll take the first watch, Ruhubi, you take the second, so get some sleep."

"Yes, my Lord," their protector replied. He rolled out his blanket near the fire and fell asleep. It took the children a little longer, but they were so tired they were soon sound asleep in the wagon with the women.

In Damascus, King Hazael found out about Naaman's departure, and ordered Ishme, Ilani, and Kapu arrested and thrown in jail.

The three prisoners heard General Ba'asa enter the building and speak to the officer in charge. "Let the three of them think about it tonight. Use torture if you have to. We must get an answer out of them. I don't care how you do it, just find out where Naaman's gone."

The guardsman on duty saluted and breathed easier once the general left.

"You heard him," he shouted at the three men chained to the wall. "You better talk." He spit on the floor, and then stormed back to his post.

"We've got to get out of here," Ishme growled.

"Under torture I'll talk, I know I will," Kapu whispered. "They'll get it out of us, you can be sure."

"I knew we should have gone with him," Ilani murmured.

"It's too late for regrets," Ishme said. No one spoke after that. Each was lost in his thoughts.

Midway through the night, a thud outside their cell awakened them. A key clanked in the lock, and the door opened.

"Hurry Captain," a friendly voice whispered.

"It's Asu," Ishme whispered, "my old sergeant."

He unlocked the men's chains. "Follow me," he ordered. Rubbing their wrists, the three friends moved out as Asu led them down a narrow street to where their horses were waiting. Men from Ishme's battalion were there holding swords, and bows and arrows.

"May the gods go with you, and give our best to the general," Asu said.

Waving to their comrades, the escapees jumped onto their horses and disappeared into the night.

CHAPTER TWENTY

YOKNEAM

On the second day of their abrupt departure from Damascus, Naaman and his fellow travelers had an encounter they would never forget. Two men were coming towards them on foot. As they drew closer, Naaman beheld a frightening sight. Both men were covered with rags. Only their eyes were visible.

The taller figure shouted, "Unclean." He and his companion moved off the road to let Naaman's party pass.

"They're lepers," Meira called out to Naaman.

Naaman's blood ran cold. He reined in his horse and motioned the wagons to stop.

"Lepers," Adorina said. She pulled Atalia closer to her.

"What are you doing, my Lord?" Captain Ruhubi said. "Let's move on."

Naaman ignored him. Instead, he dismounted and spoke to the two men. "Peace be with you, brothers." He took the money pouch from his belt and tossed it gently onto the ground at their feet. There were enough coins to feed the two men for several months.

Picking it up, the taller man looked inside. In a weak raspy voice he asked, "Why have you done this, stranger?"

Overcome by emotion, Naaman's eyes misted over, and he had trouble speaking. "In gratitude to the Lord for what he's done for me."

The other leper spoke. "The Lord will bless you."

The voice shocked Naaman because it was the voice of a woman. The man attached the money pouch to his frayed belt, and then together the lepers walked back onto the road. They continued walking slowly in the same direction as before, without as much as a glance at those behind them.

Naaman put his hands on his saddle and bowed his head. Tears rolled down his cheeks as he realized he had come face to face with the image of how his life might have ended. When he got back on his horse, no one spoke. He could tell by the faces of his family and friends that they understood what must have been going through his mind.

At noon, the little band reached the border. Levi and his wife rode up ahead since they were Israelites. And as they hoped, they met no resistance from the soldiers.

That night as they camped in the upper Galilee, Levi said, "We should reach Yokneam tomorrow afternoon dear friends."

"Things are so green here," Adorina said.

"This is only the beginning, my Lady," Levi said.

"I'll be glad when we're there," young Ashur grumbled.

Naaman would be, too. He and Levi had worried about carrying the extra money of the general's pension, and the sale Levi's house and property. They had taken precautions by hiding their coins under each of the wagons in cleverly built boxes made to resemble the undercarriage of the vehicles. They kept out only a few coins needed for daily purchases of food and wine. So far, they had encountered few travelers and only three small caravans.

Tomorrow would be the last day of the week, and the two families were eager to be in Yokneam by sunset for the start of the Sabbath. In the morning a soft rain fell, but it didn't last long.

By mid-afternoon, the wagons reached the top of a long hill and Levi suddenly shouted, "There it is," He pointed to the town nestled in the hills below.

"It's beautiful," Adorina and Meira said at the same time.

The wagons had moved slowly up the incline, but now, on the downhill, they let the horses pick up the pace. Before reaching the city gates, Levi veered off onto a side road and followed it for a short distance.

"It's just up ahead," he told them. A farmhouse came into view. They had reached their destination. A dog came running out and barked at them, followed by a young boy who saw the strangers and ran back inside. Levi drove his wagon closer to the dwelling and Naaman's family followed him.

A middle-aged man ran out of the house. "Uncle Levi, it can't be you."

Levi jumped down and embraced his nephew. "Simon. How long has it been?" Other people came out to see who had arrived and Levi introduced Naaman and his family. Simon invited them all inside.

"This will be the biggest Sabbath meal we have ever had," young Ashur said.

Naaman smiled. "And it will be the first Sabbath for us in the land of our Lord."

The family helped move the tables around until everyone had a place. Sarah, Simon's wife covered her head and prepared to light the two Sabbath candles. Suddenly the dog began barking again and footsteps were heard on the porch. The door opened and a familiar voice said, "Is there room for three more, Lord Naaman?" Ishme and his two colleagues stood there, and everyone rushed over to greet them with joy and hard slaps on the back.

"I guess we're all here now, Lady Sarah," Naaman said. "Let us praise the Lord."

"Blessed be His Name," everyone joined in.

Two months after settling at Yokneam, Naaman's family and friends finished building their new home and barn. A small separate home was built for Meira a short distance from the main house. She loved it, and so did the children who could sleep over in their own secret hideaway.

One morning, as Newman plowed a field to prepare it for his crop of wheat, he saw a wagon turn in on the road leading to his house. Giving his horse a rest, Naaman walked to the house to see who it was. A man was helping a woman down from the wagon, and when he turned, Naaman shouted, "Eleazer! I can't believe it." The two men embraced, slapping each other on the back.

"This is my wife Deborah," Eleazer said. By then, Adorina heard the wagon arrive and came out on the porch.

Naaman said, "And this is Adorina, my beloved wife."

The two women greeted each other and then went inside with the men following behind.

"I heard from one of my officers that a Syrian who had become a son of the covenant was living here. Well, I had to come, that's all there is to it. It could only be you, General."

"No longer a general, my friend," Naaman corrected. "I'm retired."

"As am I, old enemy," General Eleazer said.

"Your countrymen have made us most welcome," Naaman said. "I am content."

Eleazer suddenly had a pleased look on his face. "You know, I'm grateful to the Lord that we never had to fight each other. Who would have won, I wonder?" He grinned when he said it.

Naaman laughed. "Should we try it now, Eleazer? Hand-to-hand combat on the porch?"

"That's enough you two," Adorina said. The women brought out some cool drinks.

Eleazer and Deborah spent several weeks at Yokneam, remembering old times and sharing everything about their families and Naaman's new faith. At the end of the visit, Israelite and Syrian discovered they were very much alike.

The years passed quickly, and the prophet Elisha found himself standing in the Temple Courtyard in Jerusalem surrounded by hundreds of men waiting to hear him speak. He felt led by the Lord to the southern kingdom to reveal to their king the instructions about who would lead the country. Elisha knew that neither of the two reigning monarchs would be pleased with his declarations. His message this day was to be one of faith and the need of God's people to obey His laws and teachings.

When he finished, Shallum walked with his master away from the outer court. Someone stopped Elisha and wanted to speak with him. The prophet's companion stood aside while the two men talked. Suddenly, he overheard another conversation which drew his attention.

"How could they bring that Syrian here to the House of God?" one man said in anger. "Gentiles are forbidden in the Temple."

"Peace, Nathan," the other replied. "He was taught the faith by Elisha himself. They've taken wives among the families in Yokneam. They have every right to be here."

"Excuse me, gentlemen," Shallum said. "I am the prophet's companion and couldn't help but overhear your words about the Syrian. May I ask the man's name?"

The older man's face showed his disgust. "Naaman the leper."

Shallum wanted to smile, but controlled himself.

"Oh, you mean the Right Hand of the king and general of his army and now a son of the covenant." He wanted to remind them who Naaman had been. "Elisha and I have eaten with his family in their perfect kosher home in Damascus. The Lord has brought an important Gentile into the faith and we should praise Him for it."

"Thank you, friend of the prophet," the second man said. "Nathan meant no offense."

"Bah," the older man growled. The two men turned and hurried out of the courtyard.

"Yokneam?" Shallum repeated to himself so he wouldn't forget it. That evening at the home of a friend, he told Elisha about Naaman.

"Ah, the Lord has rescued him as I knew He would," Elisha said. "May the Lord be praised." Shallum could tell he was not at all surprised. "Yokneam you say?" Shallum nodded.

"That's my mentor Elijah's favorite place—up around Mount Carmel," Elisha continued. He began humming as he always did when he was deep in thought. "Perhaps we should give them a visit just to please me."

"And me, Master," Shallum said. "I just can't picture the general as a farmer."

"You say these men saw him in the Temple court, my son?" Elisha said.

"Yes, my Lord. "That's what made the man so angry."

"Naaman would have been one of the most sincere and faithful pilgrims there," Elisha said. "You can be sure of that."

The two holy men travelled to Yokneam, and it took them five days to reach the village. Everyone came out to greet the prophet. When the townspeople saw Elisha, they opened their homes to him, but he said, "We will stay with Naaman and his family, my friends." The elders of the village respected his decision, and Abner, the chief magistrate used his wagon to take them to the Syrian's farm.

When they reached the house late in the afternoon, only Adorina and young Hadad were inside—everyone else was still working in the fields. When she saw Abner standing at the door, she rushed to open it, thinking something must have happened. Then she saw Elisha standing beside him. She fell to the floor, prostrating herself before the holy man.

"Arise my child," Elisha said, embracing her. "Can't an old friend pay you a visit?"

She greeted Shallum and invited them both inside. Abner sensed this should be a private reunion and excused himself, taking the wagon back to town.

"Where is he?" Elisha asked.

"Out in the wheat field, my Lord," Adorina said.

Standing at the door, Elisha turned back to them. "Stay here you two." He went outside and walked through the field of grain. He could see the tall figure of his friend in the distance. He ran his hands over the tops of the wheat as he walked, savoring the scent of ripening grain.

Naaman didn't see him until the last moment. "Elisha," he shouted at the top of his lungs. He then fell onto the ground in awe.

"Stand my son." He helped Naaman up. "I have come to visit an old pupil, nothing more."

"I'm so glad," Naaman said. "We have much to tell you." As they walked back to the house, they talked happily about Elisha's journey to Yokneam and the state of the prophet's health.

That evening as everyone sat around the large tables in Naaman's front room, Namaan told Elisha everything—the flight from Damascus, betrothals, marriages and the sad death of king Hadadezer.

"The Lord has been good to you, my friends," Elisha said. "And to us as well." Everyone nodded and then he surprised them by standing.

He spoke in a deep serious voice. "Now, where is the oldest son of this house?"

Ashur stood and said, "I am here, Lord Elisha."

"I understand in a few months you will be a man and will read from the holy book. That is an important day."

"Yes my Lord," Ashur said.

"Shallum," Elisha said, pointing to his leather satchel. His servant took something out of it and handed it to him. Elisha held it up for everyone to see. It was a parchment scroll.

"A long time ago, when your father first came to this country, I gave him a scroll like this. In it were the words of Moses and your family has studied the Lord's words all these years. In this new scroll my boy, are written the songs of praise and worship written by our most glorious king—King David. Read them, study them, sing them, and teach them to your family. And may the Lord bless you Ashur, son of Naaman, friend of Elisha the Lord's prophet."

Everyone in the room wiped tears from their eyes. "Now, let's make a bonfire and have singing and dancing," Elisha said. "I feel like a celebration."

Naaman's family and friends enjoyed a good evening with the man of God. People from Simon's farm came and joined them, and Naaman had never seen the prophet laugh so much.

When the fire burned down, people excused themselves and went home to bed—first the children and their mothers, then the men who were tired from the day's hard labor. Only Naaman and his guest remained staring at the glowing embers.

"Tell me what you first thought of the Temple, my son," Elisha asked. It took Naaman a long time to describe what he saw and felt when he first entered the courtyard of the holy place.

"There were so many people," Naaman said. He tried to describe what the prophet already knew. "And the beauty of it. Solomon's design is unlike any religious structure I have ever seen. My neighbor Simon, and the others explained to me about the inside of the Most Holy Place, and how those objects represented the Light and Presence of the Lord. Adorina became jealous I think, because we men were able to be a little closer to all the places of sacrifice and worship. But she said the Court of Women was beautiful and like me, she had tears in her eyes most of the time." Naaman realized suddenly how long he had been talking, and stopped. He was pleased when he saw the approval on Elisha's face. They remained silent awhile.

Elisha watched the embers glow again as a small breeze blew over them. "The Lord has revealed to me that your army brothers will choose good wives, my son." He paused. "Well, all except Kapu, but tell him not to give up. I see a woman coming for him from the village of Gath-Hepher."

"Really, my Lord?" Naaman said. He was amused and somewhat astonished that the prophet's announcement could be so precise.

"The city elder tells me about a wonderful thing you have done, my friend. You have made it possible for a small community of lepers to make their homes near the mountain. Is this true?"

"It's something I was compelled to do," Naaman said. "How could I, whom the Lord healed of this deathly disease, not help those also afflicted? He shouldn't have told you, Master. It's a small piece of useless land where there are some caves. They can live in them and be out of the rain and cold. It is not much."

This man touched Elisha's heart. Naaman had been at the pinnacle of his Gentile world, but now worked in a field of wheat, covered with sweat. He believed the Syrian desired more than anything to praise the Lord God of Israel.

"If I had a son like you, my boy," Elisha said, "I could not be more proud. Your compassion for others and love of the Lord pleases Him and He will bless you." The elderly man stood and watched the small sparks glow as the wind blew them up into the dark sky. Turning to Naaman he spoke in a soft voice. "I will see your face no more, my son. My path is going to take me away from here. I am grateful I have been able to see the fruit of the seed the Lord planted in your heart as you stood in the Jordan River long ago. Blessed be His Name."

Naaman couldn't respond, too saddened by his mentor's words. They made their way back in silence. But before the prophet opened the door to his room, Naaman put his hand on the elderly man's arm. "Revered Teacher, may the Lord bless you and keep you tonight and always. You have honored us beyond measure."

Elisha smiled and said goodnight.

In the morning, a great crowd of field hands, neighbors and elders of the town gathered to see the prophet before he left. He stood, covered his head and prayed a special benediction upon them.

Before climbing up into the wagon, the prophet stopped and approached Naaman. "Where is Meira?" he said. "I must speak to her."

Ashur ran to bring her from the small house. The two returned a few moments later. To everyone's surprise, Elisha took her aside and whispered something in her ear before placing his hand upon her head and praying a blessing. He then embraced Lady Adorina and Naaman with great affection before climbing up into the wagon with a little help.

"Peace be with you," Naaman declared.

"And rest upon you," Elisha's said. He raised his hands in benediction. The people clapped for him as the horse pulled the wagon down the road, followed by excited children and even happier barking dogs.

When Elisha had gone Adorina sighed. "Oh I hope he comes again."

"We will not see him again, my Dear. He told me so," Naaman said.

"I pray he is wrong, Husband." They walked up the steps of their front porch where Meira waited for them.

"I'm curious, sister," Naaman said. "Can you tell us what the holy man whispered to you?"

Her face flushed red, and she acted reluctant to tell them. "Very well. Elisha said by this time next year I will be married and have a son of my own."

"Meira," Adorina shouted. "How wonderful!"

"But, my Lady," Meira whispered, now embarrassed. "I don't know any men. It isn't possible."

"No, dear friend," Naaman responded. "We of all people should know that with God all things are possible, remember?"

"Please don't say anything, friends. I'm so embarrassed."

Naaman and his wife smiled at her as they went inside. Naaman laughed. "Maybe we should have built her a bigger house."

CHAPTER TWENTY-ONE

"SHALOM"

On a cool and pleasant evening a month later, Meira made her way to Naaman's porch. She knew her friends would be sitting there enjoying the beautiful sunset. They welcomed her and invited her to join them. She sat on the front step of the porch and spent a few moments in silence. Meira tried to stay still but was unable to do so.

"I have to tell you something wonderful," she blurted out.

"Oh?" Nathan said.

"Yes. His name is Jonathan ben Nemuel." Her voice filled with excitement as she continued. "He's a distant cousin of my mother's family and he learned about me during Pentecost in Jerusalem. Somehow he heard one of the men speaking my name and told him I lived here in Yokneam."

Adorina and Naaman looked at each other and smiled. "Elisha is never wrong," Naaman said.

"We're pleased to see you so happy. When will we meet him?" Adorina asked.

"He's already here staying with Kapu," she said. "May I invite him for Sabbath supper?"

"Yes of course," Adorina said. "We'll expect him."

By the end of the month, the happy couple were not only betrothed, but married at a large wedding celebration. A week later, the groom asked to speak with Naaman. He acted nervous and out of sorts.

"I wanted to meet with you, Lord Naaman, because I've decided to take Meira home to Jammneith in the north. I have a good house and farm, but because she has been your servant, she said I must speak with you first."

Naaman nodded. After a moment he replied. "While it is true that your wife was our servant years ago, we gave her the freedom to return home at any time. She chose to stay with us and become a part of our family. I owe her my life and the children consider her an aunt and friend. When you take her from us, we will be saddened of course. She will leave an empty place in our hearts, but we are happy for you both. This is what we always wanted for her. You have our blessing, Jonathan. Make her happy."

The groom smiled. "I promise, my Lord. I know we will be happy." He bowed his head respectfully and departed.

Three days later, Naaman said farewell to their faithful friend with a promise from her that she would return each year at Passover.

Several weeks later, Kapu came to Naaman's house and the two friends sat under the large oak tree in the late afternoon. A gentle breeze rustled the leaves as they sat awhile, enjoying the moment.

His friend said, "Zeb and his wife have two new mouths to feed."

"I didn't know that."

"Yes, his nephew and niece are here. They're in their twenties I think and have come from the north. Their parents were killed in an accident on their farm and Zeb is their only living relative." Kapu paused. "The niece's name is Shoshonah and she has her eyes on me."

Naaman had to smile because Kapu said it so nonchalantly. "I'm happy for you, you old soldier. But does she know all about you? I could tell her a few things."

Kapu turned red. "She knows, General. She knows everything. And did I say she is beautiful? I wanted to ask if my friends could help me build a house. We will be betrothed next week and married after Passover."

Naaman laughed and stood. "Of course we'll help." He put his arm around his friend's shoulders. "Well, this is a happy day. I'm glad for you, my friend."

The next few weeks were pleasant. Naaman loaned Kapu the funds needed to purchase land and materials. House-raising in the country was an exciting time. The men enjoyed building a home for someone else in their community. Only Naaman knew the miraculous blessing of the marriage. Shoshonah came from the village of Gath-Helper, the very village Elisha had predicted.

Naaman's good friend Ishme had become a son of Abraham the year they arrived. He married Abigail, a cousin of their neighbor, Simon. Everyone came to help build their stone house on the land Ishme purchased. Their friend Ilani married the next year, and his bride, the niece of Levi and Rachel, built a house down the road from Naaman's farm. His old general helped him with the funds needed to purchase the land.

Even though former Captain Ruhubi had not accepted the new faith, he was asked to take charge of the local militia. The villagers liked having a professional soldier organize their defenses. A young widow found him strong and handsome and vowed she could convert him and marry him by the beginning of the new year.

Over the next ten years, life on Naaman's farm was pleasant and rewarding. Young Ashur married and moved to Jerusalem where he studied to become a teacher of the Law. Daughter Atalia married Jared, the son of the city elder. She often came to visit and brought Naaman's grandchildren—a boy and two girls.

Hadad, the eldest of Elisha's sons changed his name to Gideon with his father's permission. "As a judge in Israel, Father, Gideon became one of the greatest military commanders. I want to be like him." He joined the temple guard in the Holy City and became betrothed to the daughter of one of the priests. Their house would be in Bethany when they married.

The community of lepers at the caves of Mount Carmel were not forgotten. On a regular basis, they received building materials to construct proper houses and even do a little farming to sustain themselves. Even though Naaman still tried to give anonymously, the lepers knew it was he who sent everything.

The next year Naaman buried his beloved Adorina. She had developed a cough during the cold winter months and could not get rid of it. Naaman hired physicians from all over the region, even Jerusalem, but she did not get better.

One evening, when she couldn't sleep he sat beside her on the bed and they talked about old times, their children, and what she wanted him to do if anything happened to her.

She whispered. "I'm so glad Meira could come with Jonathan and their twin boys." Her voice had become raspy from the persistent cough.

"I couldn't keep her away, Beloved," Naaman said.

"And Atalia and the children, I don't know how they could get away. You shouldn't have made them come." Her husband didn't respond because his voice would have betrayed him so he simply nodded and held her hand. He filled their bed chamber with bouquets of flowers—the red poppies she loved and some of her carefully cultivated roses. Wild lilies added a sweet perfume. Their pure whites and yellows were the colors she loved. "There are many more flowers in Israel," she would always say, comparing the land where she grew up and her new home.

"Have you been happy all these years, my Love" she asked him.

"Such a question," Naaman whispered. "I have been in heaven, or as close to heaven as I could be with one of the Lord's angels to love and care for me. Such a question, Adorina."

She smiled and wanted to laugh, but knew that would start her coughing again.

"And you, Dearest of my heart? Have you been happy?" he asked.

She squeezed his hand. "Such a question indeed. I too have been in our very own Garden of Eden, with the best 'Adam' on earth. We have been given three children to love—well, perhaps four if you count Meira—and such adults they have become. I've been shown a faith and a God to love and serve—our lives have been good." She motioned for some water and he handed her a cup and helped her sip from it.

"Enough talk for now," he said, getting off the bed, but she held onto his hand.

"Promise me you'll let me rest here on the farm when the Lord takes me." She whispered it as if it were a prayer.

"Enough talk, Dorina, but I promise, and you must do the same for me."

"I will, my General," she said, using her favorite title for him. "I will."

"Good," he said, as he bent over and kissed her on the lips.

When he awoke the next morning, he discovered she had died in her sleep. He tore his robe and all of Yokneam mourned with him. He buried her under the oak tree in the field where she loved to sit and sew and watch the workers tilling the soil around her.

Five years later, Naaman joined her, and people from all over the country came to see his tomb. Meira, Ishme, Ilani, and Kapu were inconsolable and even Naaman's children tried without success to bring them out of their sadness.

A monument of stone stood next to Lady Adorina's grave. Naaman's children had a hard time deciding what to inscribe on the headstone. These are the words they finally chose:

Naaman,
Warrior, Husband, Father
Friend of Elisha.
Your ways, O God are holy,
What god is so great as our God?
You are the God Who performs miracles;
You display your power among the peoples.

For many generations after his death, small memorial stones were left at the foot of the ancient tomb. There were so many, they were made into a memorial pillar. They were brought by the people of the small community of lepers at Mount Carmel, and were placed there to honor Naaman, the leper.

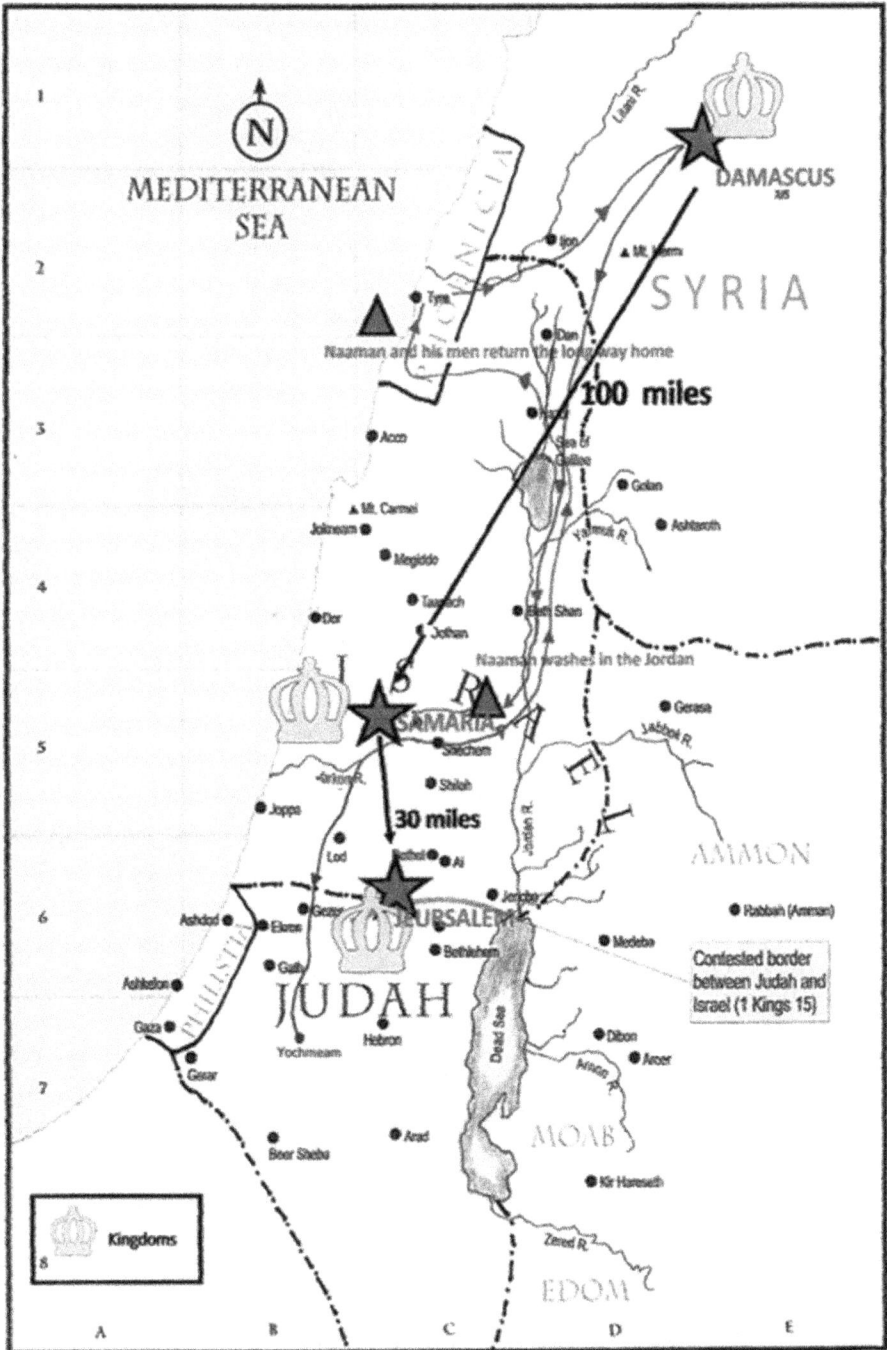

www.ingramcontent.com/pod-product-compliance
Lightning Source LLC
Chambersburg PA
CBHW032117040426
42449CB00005B/176